D1044876

Pulling Up Roots

PULLING UP ROOTS

**For Young Adults
and Their Parents—
Letting Go and
Getting Free**

Quentin F. Schenk
Emmy Lou Schenk

A SPECTRUM BOOK

Prentice-Hall, Inc., Englewood Cliffs, New Jersey 07632

Library of Congress Cataloging in Publication Data

Schenk, Quentin F.
    Pulling up roots.

    (A Spectrum Book)
    Includes bioliographies and index.
    1. Young adults—United States.   2. Maturation
(Psychology)   3. Young adults—Conduct of life.
4. Parent and child.   I. Schenk, Emmy Lou, joint
author.   II. Title.
HQ799.7.S25   301.43'15'0973   78-1873
ISBN 0-13-740423-9
ISBN 0-13-740415-8 pbk.

© 1978 by Prentice-Hall, Inc., Englewood Cliffs, N.J. 07632

A SPECTRUM BOOK

Printed in the United States of America

10 9 8 7 6 5 4 3 2 1

PRENTICE-HALL INTERNATIONAL, INC., *London*
PRENTICE-HALL OF AUSTRALIA PTY., LIMITED, *Sydney*
PRENTICE-HALL OF CANADA, LTD., *Toronto*
PRENTICE-HALL OF INDIA PRIVATE, LIMITED, *New Delhi*
PRENTICE-HALL OF JAPAN, INC., *Tokyo*
PRENTICE-HALL OF SOUTHEAST ASIA PTE., LTD., *Singapore*
WHITEHALL BOOKS, LIMITED, *Wellington, New Zealand*

In memory of Fred

Acknowledgements

We wish to thank Joan Chalmers, a one-person cheering section; Joyce Dobberpuhl, who translated our hieroglyphics into the typewritten word; and Alex Haeuser, who organized our classes for parents. The encouragement of parents gave us confidence that we had sufficient to say to make it worth the effort to put it in writing. Pat, Karl, Dirk, our two Marthas, and their many friends provided the insights that made the book possible.

Contents

7

Moving Toward Adulthood:
NQA's and Career Establishment

8

Moving Toward Adulthood:
Establishing Adult Relationships
Between Children and Parents

Pulling Up
Roots

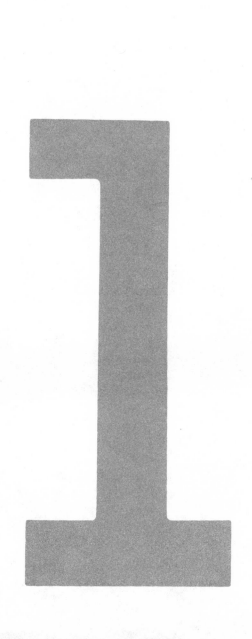

Who
Are
the
NQA's?

Much writing, discussion, and speculation have been done about the characteristics of young persons, from the time of birth through high-school years. The Freudians, behaviorists, clergy, and numerous self-styled experts have expounded upon the mental, physical, and emotional problems that parents may encounter in raising a family. Indeed, there is almost no aspect of child rearing, no matter how intimate or esoteric, that has not been discussed in both scholarly and popular media. There is advice readily available on bed-wetting, thumb-sucking, the first day in school, sexual beginnings, acne, the slow learner, and on and on. Parents may not necessarily find answers to their particular problems, but they can always find the comfort of knowing that others have experienced the same problems and have managed to live through them.

This outpouring comes to an abrupt halt for parents whose children have reached the age of 18. It is as though there were no crucial family relationships to be worked out after the high school years, no experiences to be shared, no problems to be discussed, and no joys to culminate one's parental tasks, for what little is said is negative. The generation gap is presented as so unbridgeable that one might just as well forget the whole business and go play golf. On the other hand, the advice, when it is given, sometimes seems based on the same set of assumptions given in the manuals for what to do when an eight-year-old fails to make the Little League team.

A psychologist on a TV talk show unwittingly provided more evidence of the need for a book such as this. A parent in the audience was concerned about his 23-year-old son. The young man spent four years in the navy and was now discharged. He had been at home for two months and seemed quite content to stay. He was not looking for work or making plans for further education, and the parent was wondering how best to edge the son out into the world again. The psychologist answered that the main thing was to make sure that the "child" (the psychologist's word) should not be made to feel unwanted.

This young man was not a veteran of trenches or foxholes; he had not been a victim of tortures as a POW; he was not wounded either emotionally or physically. He had been independent for four years as a uniformed employee of the U.S. government, and now he was home, lying around the house with no apparent purpose in life. As an individual, he was not unwanted or unloved. The parents already had allowed him a two-month "vacation." They were asking how they could encourage this young man to act like an adult, without destroying the relationship. What they got was an answer that might have been taken from an article on how to live through the first day of kindergarten without undue trauma.

The parents probably came away feeling that they were the only people in the world experiencing this difficulty; certainly the only ones who didn't know how to handle it.

Yet, consider the large number of young persons from about ages 18–25 who are now struggling to work out their lives, especially in relation to their parents. Consider the large number of parents who are attempting to work out their relationships to these young people who happen to be their sons and daughters. This period of life, from the end of legal dependence to the time when young persons are no longer dependent upon the home of origin for emotional, social, and financial support, largely has been neglected by contemporary experts in the "family watching" field. However, this period is very important from the standpoint of both parents and the young people.

These are the NQA's, the "not quite adolescents," the "not quite adults."

Emergence of NQA's

It is not surprising that so little attention has been given to NQA's, for they have only recently appeared upon the American scene. Social historians[1] trace the development of our society from one that was largely rural to one that is urban-industrial. In rural society, children were an economic asset. They usually left their dependent status in the home after an abbreviated adolescence. They stayed in the home only if they could be of benefit economically; otherwise they went out to find work. In a labor-intensive society, all hands were needed. But a labor-intensive society did not last long in a rapidly industrializing United States.

The child labor laws of the early part of this century can be seen not only as humanitarian acts, but also as legal recognition that children were becoming less valuable economically. As industrialization proceeded, jobs became further limited and were more tightly claimed by the adults. In order to manage the children during an ever-extending childhood, compulsory education was extended. Schools can very well be viewed in part as labor-holding pools for the otherwise excess labor available to our society. If all the young persons now in school were defined as an unemployed segment of the labor market, our unemployment rate would be, by this redefinition, chronically much higher. One of the very powerful forces, then, to extend dependency through the NQA years is the continuing process set loose with industrialization to define youth at a higher and higher age as surplus labor; and therefore, dependent upon home, school, and community for a longer and longer period of time.

Over the past century we have learned to live with the phenomenon of adolescence. We have built means of dealing with the situation through the emphasis upon compulsory education, summer camps, recreation centers, the automobile, and part-time work. But with the extension of dependent status to the NQA group, societal resources have not yet developed sufficiently to accommodate this segment of our population. As a result, stresses appear, which are defined as problems by society. Eventually, no doubt the NQA's will be accommodated in society, as the adolescent group has been. Until that happens conflicts concerning the NQA's will remain with us.

"Not Quiteness" Described

At present the NQA years are marked with inconsistencies.[2] NQA men and women are at the peak of their physical prowess, yet they are defined as youth or kids and, except for the athletes, often regarded as unfit for anything other than menial tasks. They are required to fight our wars, yet they are just beginning to become universally franchised. Even so, they cannot hold all public offices because of age limitations. It is possible for them to be socially and psychologically independent of their families, most of their loyalties going to members of their own age groups. Yet, most NQA's are forced by society to be economically dependent upon their families or some social or governmental agency. They have many choices concerning eventual occupations, but, except for jobs that have a limited opportunity for advancement, they must undergo an extended training period with no guarantee of vocational success. They are singled out by law enforcement agencies, insurance companies, and others as a high-risk group, and therefore marginal to the adult community.

NQA's are told to exercise their freedom, and when they do—by dressing their own way, having their own argot, developing their own dance and art forms—they are criticized or laughed at by adults. NQA's desire to spend their money their own way, but since some of what they have comes from sources other than their own adult labor, they have strings attached to the use of their money. In short, at the present time the NQA's find themselves in a period of marked inconsistencies and confusion.

The Importance of Family Relationships

A number of important commentators on the family[3,4] have written that the relationships between parents and children are of utmost importance from birth to age 6 or to age 12, depending upon the individual commentator. However, the authors believe that all the years are important for parents and their children. These relationships should be seen as a continuum from the early years, when parents take complete responsibility, to the NQA years, when a tenuous bond of responsibility and control still exists, a bond that soon will be diffused even further.

The NQA period is one of personal reintegration for both parents and their children. For the parents, it is a time that culminates in the loss of control, which began when their children left home to attend kindergarten or first grade. It is

also a time when parents look forward to the end of the pro-
longed economic responsibility they assumed when the children were born.

For NQA's it is the opposite. They are being forced to
move from irresponsibility to responsibility. They can no
longer be certain that, whatever they do, parents will take
over and straighten it out for them, particularly when the
going gets rough. The opportunity to "cop out" onto parents
decreases with the passing of each day. NQA's can no longer
count on parents to be their backstops. Indeed, NQA's are
sometimes asked to do a little backstopping themselves.

Parents may be expected to furnish some financial assistance, but the dichotomy is becoming clearer. The former
home of both parents and children is gradually becoming the
parents' home, which the NQA's can still use, but more selec-
tively. The car is available, but with more and more conditions attached to its use, and NQA's are expected to obtain
their own transportation. When money is available, it is for a
specified use for a limited time, and even the source is slowing
to a trickle.

Young people say that home is the place where you can
go when nobody else wants you. The awful possibility now
looms on the horizon for them that this haven of safety no
longer may be provided by the parents.

The protracted procedure of parental emancipation and
attainment of adulthood is said to be full of pitfalls and prat-
falls, and is often looked upon with dread. Parents enjoy
being needed by their children; there are seminars on how to
handle the "empty nest" syndrome. Children want to be dependent on their parents; note the young man from the service. But all "want" in their own ways and according to their
own definitions. Thus, each contingent has a problem—the
children to hang on to the good deal they have always had,
and the parents to prevent the loss of dependents, whose
control, care, and love they have so long enjoyed.[5]

Each contingent dreads the day when the relationship is
irreversibly altered; when parents must reconcile themselves

to a life of less intimacy with the children; when children must accept that they make it or blow it on their own, with no backup from parents. It is this sense of impending developments that contributes to the issues that arise between parents and children during the NQA period.

The NQA period is probably the most volatile of all the years in which parents and children relate to each other. Society expects NQA's to take those final steps to become equals to, or better than, their parents, and no longer to be dependent upon them as before. These steps are taken in three categories: *financial*, *social*, and *emotional*. These are the major categories of relationships within which members of families interact. The issue, therefore, is not the kinds of relationships that exist between NQA's and parents, but the manner in which they exist and the struggle to recast them into forms that imply equality rather than dependency.

Financial Dependence and Independence

NQA's have, up to this point in their lives relied primarily upon parents for food, transportation, telephone, clothing, cleaning, spending money, health care, money for leisure pursuits, and so on. Now it begins to become apparent to the NQA's that this well has a bottom to it. They must learn to replace this source, and the preparation to do so is one of the overriding concerns of this period. This is accomplished in a variety of ways, discussed in the later chapters.

Social Dependence and Independence

Children position themselves in relation to their friends and acquaintances with reference to the position their parents have in the community. If a parent has a professional occupation, children will see themselves in the socioeconomic context in which that profession is placed. If a parent comes from an old respected family, children will expect the same kind of respect for themselves. At the point of becoming NQA's most young persons begin to realize that they must develop their own social positions or status based on their own achievements rather than on that of their parents. It can be a frightening realization for both parents and NQA's, for they must consider, for the first time, that society offers opportunities for both upward and downard mobility.

Emotional Dependence
and Independence

When a little child has stubbed a toe or been called names by the bully on the street, comfort is usually offered by the parents until the child feels emotionally whole again. When a child is lonely, parents can be counted on to try to make the child feel part of a group again. When flushed with success because of some achievement, it is the parents' praise that the child seeks first. For NQA's, all this is no longer sufficient. Parents cannot provide exclusive support for the hurts and loneliness, or praise for kudos. Whether or not they are close at hand, they are no longer the NQA's most important reference group. Emotional independence cannot be achieved by NQA's until they have sources of emotional support other than their parents.

Moving Toward Adulthood

If parents want to teach a child how to swim, they can provide lessons so that swimming can be learned in an orderly, logical fashion, or they can throw the youngster off the end of the dock and see what happens. Also, there are parents who think that swimming is entirely too dangerous, and they will forbid their children to go anywhere near the water.

Since the NQA period has recently emerged, working

out the dependencies has been accomplished mainly by the "sink or swim" or "don't go near the water" methods. Parents seldom had the know-how or took the time to develop a logical, orderly approach that could help them work through the NQA period for the benefit of all concerned. Instead of "kicking the damn kid out" (sink or swim approach) or "hanging on as long as possible" (don't go near the water approach), we will consider the third option (the teaching approach) in later chapters. We will discuss reasons that problems arise and will offer solutions that can be helpful to parents and NQA's.

Many family watchers tell us that the family is coming apart at the seams, that it isn't what it used to be in the "good old days."[6] These people regard changes in the family as synonymous with breakdown, which the authors feel is far from the case. Many changes have taken place in our society and are still taking place, and the family must adjust to them. The fact that families do make these adjustments is proof of strength, not weakness, even if stress is evident. The family formerly had much less importance during young adulthood than it does today.

This extended period of NQA dependence is a problem in many families for two reasons: the inability of NQA's to be completely free from a dependent relationship on the parents, and the parents' lack of desire to let go of their NQA's.

These are the reasons for this book—to examine the changes, to show specifically how they are felt in family relationships, and to offer suggestions as to how these relationships can be managed so that families may continue to serve their members effectively.

REFERENCES

[1]D. Riesman, *The Lonely Crowd* (New Haven: Yale University Press, 1961).

[2]H. Dimock, *Rediscovering the Adolescent* (New York: Association Press, 1947).

[3]I. Josselyn, *Psychosocial Development of Children* (New York: Family Service Assn. of America, 1948).

[4]A. Gesell, *The First Years of Life* (New York: Harper, 1940).

[5]R. LaPiere, *The Freudian Ethic* (New York: Duell, Sloan, & Pearce, 1959), Chap. 4.

[6]David Cooper, *The Death of the Family*. (New York: Random House, Pantheon Books, 1970).

FOR ADDITIONAL READING

"Adulthood" *Daedulus*, in *Journal of the American Academy of Arts & Science*, Spring 1976.

Youth: Transition to Adulthood. Report of the Panel on Youth of the President's Science Advisory Committee. U.S.G.P.O., June 1973.

The books above offer a wide variety of points of view by a number of authors on older youth and early adulthood.

SHEEHY, G., *Passages: Predictable Crises of Adult Life*. New York: E.P. Dutton, 1976.

A popular statement of the periods that individuals in modern society traverse, emphasizing the difficulties of transition from one to the other.

The Struggle
for Control—
The Struggle
for Autonomy

In the United States, children are often assumed to be the exclusive possession of their parents.[1] Since parents often feel they "own" their children, they also often feel they have exclusive control over children's behavior and the responsibility for that behavior. Parents would like to have the same kind of control over their children as they would over any other property they might own. This expectation is usually fulfilled when children are young and have not yet acquired a highly developed self-concept. When they do acquire a more individualized view of themselves and a sense of their own autonomy, they cease to be passive objects in the hands of parents. At this point, a struggle for control becomes apparent, one that continues throughout the period during which children are dependent upon their parents.

Who Calls the Shots?

Society fails to take into account that the legal power parents can use to back up their control of children comes to an abrupt halt when the children reach the age of majority—18 in most states. Most discussion and writing about family relationships does not concern how parents might use their authority over their children to effect the transition from childhood to adulthood.

Even Thomas Gordon in *P. E. T., Parent Effectiveness Training*,[2] who discusses the ineffectiveness of power-oriented relationships and the fact that parents do not really "own" their children, still uses as examples situations in which the parents want to get the child to do something—get to school on time without complaints, wear a raincoat, go to bed without an argument, come in at a certain hour, and so on. Parents who learn to be "effective" by this system utilize a permissive system for controlling their children's behavior, but the purpose is still to control the child's behavior.

In the *P. E. T.* manual, as in other child-rearing books, little attention is paid to understanding the social situations in which the techniques are to be applied. There is no description of the hoped for outcome of the parenting years. It is little wonder that parents do not recognize that their children are unlike any other "possessions" they may have; ultimate success comes at the time when parents can say, "You no longer belong to me. You are not my responsibility. You belong to yourself and are your own responsibility." The propriety view that parents have toward their children results in confusion about who belongs to whom and how much at what place and when. Parents' struggle for control versus NQA's struggle for autonomy comes to a climax during the NQA period.

Authoritarianism

Parents often try to control their NQA's by use of authoritarian means that might have worked when the children were much younger. As an example: Marge was living at home and working as a clerk in a store. Her parents ruled her every movement, which she never seemed to mind until she became interested in a young man from another ethnic group. She began to spend much of her free time with him to the consternation of her authoritarian parents. Soon Marge and her parents were arguing over Marge's boy friend, and her parents refused to let Marge see him. They tried to restrict her phone calls and her free time, but they found that they could not do so. One ultimatum generated another, and one day Marge packed and left home. She moved in with the young man. Her parents were horrified to discover that legally Marge had every right to do so and that the authority the parents thought they had was imaginary. Even more important, now they had also lost their ability to influence Marge's behavior through their relationship with her.

Permissiveness

At the other extreme are parents who try to exert control over NQA's by being permissive. Some do so because they feel guilty if they deny the wishes of their children or fail to meet their demands because they believe that in so doing they will inhibit their emotional development. Other parents misinterpret the generation gap theories. They think that their ideas are outdated and that the children have all the answers for life in a brave new culture they are developing. Others have been so manipulated by their children that their attempts to control are ineffectual. Whatever the reason, and there are many not mentioned, by the time of the NQA period, these permissive parents follow the line of least resistance. They want to define acceptable behavior for their children as much as do the authoritarian parents. They just go at it in a different way.

For example: Tom graduated from high school and went away to college. During his freshman year, he failed to make satisfactory grades. He spent the money he had been allotted and borrowed more from his parents. Finally he was suspended from school; he came home and got a job. His parents allowed him to live at home without paying room and board or requiring him to help in any way with the household chores, nor did they make him pay back the money he had borrowed the previous year.

Tom saved enough money from his salary and his parents' indulgence to make a down payment on a car. The parents cosigned his loan for the balance due and also loaned him more money to pay the first installment on his insurance. One day Tom took a trip in his car, and later that day Tom's parents received a call from the police. Tom had been in an accident and had left the scene. No one was injured, but Tom had damaged another car. He was in big trouble! Tom, of course, had an explanation for what he had done, which the parents did not question. They hired a lawyer for him, and in the end he received a short jail sentence and a stiff fine, which the parents paid.

Tom is still living at home, going to a local college now and doing poorly. His mother drives him to school and also to work. She spends a great deal of time worrying about his behavior, but neither parent can see that there is anything he or she might do to improve that behavior. As soon as Tom's license is renewed, they plan to buy him another car.

On a day-to-day basis, it might seem as though Tom has it made since his parents do everything for him. But, in fact, they cannot let go, for they see Tom as their child to be taken care of and protected as if he were seven or eight. Tom probably wants to get free, but he cannot, for he has allowed himself to be bought out by his parents. He may stay an NQA forever.

Many parents vacillate between authoritarianism and

permissiveness, and are unsatisfied with the results. They swing from treating NQA's as though they were still little children to acting as if the NQA's were their adult peers. Neither parents nor NQA's know where they stand in relationship to each other, and the result is a mixture of confusion, anxiety, hostility, and continued dependency.

From One Extreme to the Other—
The Ping-Pong Parents

When Irv graduated from high school, his parents promised him part-ownership in the family business when he finished college. Obediently, Irv went off to study business administration. He did well during his first year, but his parents worried about what radical or otherwise evil things he might be learning along with business administration. So, when a recession decreased the family profits, the parents used that as an excuse to keep Irv at home. He went to work in the family business, used the family car, and, since he lived at home, invited his friends in to visit.

Soon conflicts developed, and one day, with little warning, Irv's parents asked him to get his own place to live. Obediently, Irv moved into his own apartment. Soon after, he began to date a young woman. He fell in love and told his parents he wished to marry. His parents had no objection to the particular young woman, but they thought Irv was too young to get married. They felt they could control him if he lived at home, so they began to put pressure on Irv to move back. When he was less obedient than usual, they told him they would not give him the share in the family business unless he did as they said.

Irv resisted for a while, but he finally moved back into

the home. Soon his relationship with the young woman ended, and Irv became socially dependent on his parents. Today, two years later, Irv's parents still have not formally given him a share in the business, but they keep promising that they will.

Irv's parents do not know whether to treat Irv as a young child, their own property, or as a maturing adult, an independent person. They vacillate between the two extremes, with the result that they have a son who is unable to break away, yet feels the stress of not being able to mature, to get free from his parents, or to create his own resources. Irv's parents do not understand why their son is not content with his situation, especially since they feel that they have done so much for him in the past and are continuing to provide for him.

It may seem here that parents are "damned if they do and damned if they don't," and that since there is no good way to control the behavior of the NQA, parents might just as well forget it. If control is defined as the ability to manipulate children as though they were stoves or lawnmowers, then perhaps this might be true. Surely it is best for both parents and NQA's to let go of the need for this kind of control.

The NQA period offers the potential for parents to influence the NQA's future in significant ways. This potential is still very much there even if absolute control is no longer desirable or possible. Parents must learn to recognize when and how they are still influencing their NQA's and the methods they can use for doing so in a positive rather than a negative fashion. For, although parents can no longer control the NQA's, they do control themselves and their own resources. NQA's can use this period to learn the differences between parental behavior that hinders or helps. It is through this realization on the part of parents and NQA's that positive influences can be exerted.

There are a number of areas where issues arise in parent–NQA relationships. These areas are possessions, territory, status, and emotional support.

Possessions

Our social values permit parents to see their children as exclusive possessions. This causes conflicts between parents and NQA's over the ownership and use of the material goods that are part of the family resources.

Permissive parents view ownership and use by children in the same light as they view ownership and use by themselves. They see all possessions of the family as belonging to all members of the family.

Authoritarian parents see children as their property in the same way they see an automobile or a television set as their property. They attempt to manipulate their NQA's behavior as they would any other object over which they wish to have control.

Either approach hinders the development of an NQA's independence. Both make it difficult for parents to see their possessions as separate from the possessions of NQA's and to enforce this separation. In either case it becomes more difficult for NQA's to break away from being participating members of the intimate family group, a break that is mandatory if the NQA's are to become fully participating adults in society.

Both permissive and authoritarian parents sometimes try to use possessions to control specific behavior of NQA's, a sort of bribe approach. For instance, they permit the NQA to use the family car only after doing the dishes, mowing the lawn, or promising not to drink or not to go out with a particular young person because the parents disapprove.

One twenty-year-old had transformed his mother's car into a junker through a series of minor accidents, and the insurance costs had gone to astronomical heights. He had taken the car without asking and left his mother stranded. The young man had taken his girl friend out, and the car had been parked in front of her home till early morning (a helpful neighbor had reported). The mother was suspicious that he was drinking and driving at the same time, maybe even smoking pot or worse. The list of woes went on and on. Added to them all he never helped around the house.

Some questioning brought out the fact that the son had nearly $700.00 in the bank. "Why," she was asked in amazement, "do you let him drive your car since he gives you so much grief with it? Can't he get his own car?"

"Oh, you don't understand," she replied. "The car is the only way we can control him."

Parents with this perception fail to realize that NQA's have an autonomy conferred upon them by their age that makes it impossible to exert the kind of control the parents desire. This mother cannot ride in the back seat of the car every time her son is in it to make sure that he is living up to his promises, that he is not driving too fast, or drinking, or parking with his girl friend. Parents who push too far the use of their possessions to control the behavior of NQA's will become frustrated and possibly embittered, for NQA's behavior can no longer be controlled except by NQA's themselves.

Possessions are crucial. It is in this area that the most obvious conflicts occur because this is where NQA's put up the greatest resistance to being independent. If Johnny has been allowed to use the family car whenever he wants, with or without conditions placed upon its use, he will want to stay dependent upon the family because he is unable to buy himself such an expensive car. If Susie gets money any time she asks for it, she will resist being cut off from the source of supply. Many of the NQA's who wander about aimlessly sifting through career choices and goals as though they were window shopping do so because their parents have given them no reason to take responsibility for providing their own material resources.

Parents and NQA's should recognize that family possessions are, in fact, not *family* possessions at all. What Mom and Dad have worked for, acquired, and cared for over the years belongs to Mom and Dad, and NQA's must begin to accumulate their own possessions as they are able.

Of course, since parents control the use of their possessions, it is possible for them to set down any conditions they wish to make upon that use. Parents can even wait up until six a.m. to see if the twenty-year-old smells of alcohol, and then say, "You've been drinking again. How many times do we have to tell you not to? Okay, now you don't get to use the car for two weeks. Maybe that will teach you a lesson." From the standpoint of the car, they have that option since they own the car. However, since they do not own the NQA, this option is no longer viable. The parent who does this is trying to control both the person and the possessions, and this becomes less practical every year.

The separation of parents' and NQA's possessions should be established by the parents setting rules only for the *way in which* the possessions are used. For instance, parents might permit the NQA to have a party for friends provided the NQA buys the food, cleans up the kitchen and whatever other rooms are used, and sees to it that the guests don't break up the furniture. The NQA should understand that careless use of parents' possessions or no cleanup will put an end to party giving. There is no point in saying that the NQA can have the party provided no guest smokes pot; that condition could be enforced only by the parents' constant presence at the party. Even then, one cannot know for sure that nobody stood out on the porch and smoked. Parents can control the use that NQA's make of the parents' possessions by withdrawing their permission for use whenever they wish, but they should recognize that they control only the *way* things are used, not the *behavior* of the user.

If the NQA is allowed use of the family car, he or she should pay for the gasoline and oil that is used. Working NQA's should pay their share of the cost of insurance and maintenance. If the NQA has an accident, he or she should pay the deductible and the increase in the insurance costs that may result. In short, NQA's should learn that if they make use of another person's possessions (in this case, the parents') they must be responsible for that use.

It is not easy for parents and NQA's to recognize that parents have control over use of possessions, particularly if NQA's have been allowed to take this use for granted at an earlier period. Some parents also have difficulty learning the other side of the coin—NQA's have possessions that the parents cannot use. How easy it is for parents to forget this, to borrow without asking permission, for if parents believe that the child belongs to them, then the child's things belong to them too.

When parents do not take the initiative to control their own possessions and do no separate children from the category of possessions, barriers are established in developing the kind of autonomy that is necessary if NQA's are to become truly adult.

Territory

NQA's consume much space and tend to have a feeling of unilateral territorial rights. They often scatter their clothes over most of the house, especially the bathroom. Some take their car apart in the garage and leave junk scattered around so there is no room for the family car. Others bring their friends into the family room and take over. They may use Dad's desk and Mom's sewing room as their own. They might cook in the kitchen and dirty the dishes. They look for clothes in their parents' closets, and all the time they seem unaware that they are invading someone else's territory.

In fact, personal territory *is* a possession, but it goes beyond the strictly material aspect that we used to define possessions. Personal territory is spatial as well as material. To be a successful and happy adult, persons must be able to differentiate between exclusive, shared, and unavailable territories. Adults have personal territories reserved for their exclusive use, such as their house, their yard, kitchen and equipment, workbench and the tools that go with it. They also have rights to the use of territory in conjunction with others; to share the streets, space in stores, public buildings, and churches, and so on. Finally, some territory is restricted from their use. Other persons' homes, others' mates, reserved radio frequencies, the White House—generally, these are all unavailable territory.

The proper use of territory in the home is the best way for NQA's to learn this concept. It also makes life a lot easier for all concerned. Unfortunately, parents do not always make clear which territories in the home fall into which category

Permissive parents, who feel that everything belongs to everyone, allow their children to use all areas of the house without restriction, even though this may cause considerable inconvenience. Authoritarian parents go through their children's drawers and open their mail on the grounds that everything belongs to the parents, including any thing or person within their boundaries. As we said before, these approaches may not have caused trouble when the children were younger, but they become completely untenable at the NQA period. The spatial requirements of NQA's increase, as anyone knows who has tried to fit a car into the place where the bicycle used to go, and NQA's no longer will tolerate the intrusions into their privacy that an adolescent permitted. In any event, if it has not been done before, it is time for NQA's to be given a room or portion of a room that is for their use alone. No one else should use that space in any way without the permission of its owner. This is the NQA's exclusive territory.

Some areas of the home should be forbidden to the NQA—perhaps Dad's favorite chair, the parents' liquor cabinet, other family members' bedrooms and closets, and so on. This is unavailable territory.

The rest of the home may be considered shared territory, available for the use of the NQA provided he or she respects the rights of others who are also users. An example might be permission to use part of the garage provided that space is left for the parents' car.

Time and territory are closely related. The NQA period is usually one of intense self-preoccupation, the result of which is the NQA's assumption that his or her interests are automatically the interests of the parents. NQA's often feel that parents are "so old" that they never do anything that matters anyway, so they think parents always should be ready to drop whatever they are doing and give their undivided time to their NQA's. This is more likely to be a problem with those NQA's who live outside the home and turn up occasionally for visits or vacations. It is often difficult for NQA's to accept the idea that parents may have, in the NQA's absence, developed their own activities and problems, and are not necessarily eager to take the time to do whatever it is that the NQA has in mind for them to do.

NQA's tend to call on Sunday and say, "Good news. I can come home on Tuesday instead of Friday, so come and get me then." They cheerfully ignore the fact that it might be inconvenient or even impossible for the parents to make a 200-mile round trip with no advance scheduling. Or they might come home unexpectedly because it is a good afternoon—as far as the NQA's are concerned—for Dad to help them fix the car or because a party dress needs fitting to be worn on Saturday night. They sometimes act as though parents are just sitting around waiting for the NQA's to provide a little fun and amusement in their dreary lives.

Unless NQA's learn that time is a nonmaterial resource that each person controls for his or her own use, as well as for others, and unless parents insist that NQA's understand and respect this, then NQA's will continue to see parents' time as synonymous with their own. NQA's still have a right to some undivided time with parents, but only as parents choose to give that time to them. It is important for NQA's to learn to use time in an adult way, to differentiate among exclusive time, shared time, and unavailable time in the same way that territory and possessions are differentiated.

Status

A child's family is important in determining what position the child will have when he or she becomes an adult. This is not to say that children will automatically obtain a position in society equal to that of their parents. With talent, work, perseverance, and luck, they can be upwardly mobile. Without these, they may be downwardly mobile. However, the family is the launching pad for adult achievement.

Children take for granted their position in the community, and they seldom realize how much it is related to their family's position. Where they live, the school or church they attend, the friends they play with, what they read, where they travel are all related to their family status. If the family is highly valued in the community, children generally will be accorded positive responses. If the family is not highly regarded, the children will tend to have low morale, low motivation, and low feelings of self-esteem.

Parents' perceptions of their positions in the community have a powerful influence on the aspirations of NQA's. If parents feel a necessity for their children to occupy a better position in life than they did, NQA's will be under parental pressure to perform in order to achieve that position. If parents already see themselves in a position in the community in accordance with their own aspirations, they will attempt to ensure that their NQA's also occupy that position. Parents will use their influence with their friends to obtain breaks for their NQA's, such as job opportunities, introductions to the proper people who can assist NQA's with their future, and they will exhort NQA's to be as successful as they possibly can.

It is in the drive for status that parents place the most pressure on NQA's. Those who have let go in other ways often feel that they fave failed as parents if their children do not achieve the position in life that parents think they should achieve.

To assist NQA's to achieve a social position most satisfying to all concerned, parents should expect NQA's to do as much as they can on their own. Parents should assist them only in what they are as yet unable to achieve by themselves. But here, as well as in the other issues of control and discipline, parents should separate their aspirations from those of NQA's. If this separation does not take place, frustration and friction will result.

As an example: Boyd's father is the manager of a large factory. He has no college education, and he spent his boyhood during the Depression. He vividly remembers the hardship he endured and considers his present success due largely to his efforts to escape his boyhood position. Boyd is 20 and is content to work in his father's factory. But his father is not content. He keeps badgering Boyd to go to a high prestige college, but when Boyd decided he would like to go to a local technical school, his father refused to pay the tuition. It wasn't good enough.

The father has threatened to disown Boyd if he does not achieve what his father aspires for him. At the same time, he gives Boyd all manner of assistance so that Boyd can continue to enjoy the same standard of living and status in the community. He has bought him a car and gives him money beyond his salary. When Boyd moved out of the home, his father found a "proper" apartment for him and pays his rent. Boyd has recognized what a good deal he has and now does just barely enough to keep his father believing that there is still a hope that Boyd will eventually accomplish his father's expectations. At present, Boyd has a nearly free ride. The odds are that Boyd's father will continue this same pattern until he separates his ambitions for himself from those that Boyd has for himself.

It would be much better for Boyd's father to recognize what is happening to himself and to Boyd, and to let Boyd go. He cannot because he sees Boyd only as an extension of himself. He is unable to allow Boyd a life of his own. It also would be better for Boyd to get free of his father and to realize that by continuing his free ride he is, in fact, prolonging a childlike relationship with his father. Both father and son are contributing equally to the continuance of an immature relationship from which each is unable to let go or get free.

Al's story is different. His maternal grandfather was a naval officer, as was his father. Both of his parents wanted him to choose the navy as a career, and they encouraged him to go to the Naval Academy. Al was much interested in sports in high school. He saw the Academy as a place where this interest could be pursued. By the combined efforts of the parents and Al in writing congressmen, contacting persons acquainted with the Academy, and taking tests, Al was admitted. He was enthusiastic about plebe summer, but his ardor began to cool during the first semester of his freshman year, for he recognized something that he had not seen before. The Naval Academy has a primary mission to train engineers for the navy. Al did not want to be an engineer. Al's parents urged him to stay because of the family tradition, and so Al tried the second semester. After a month, he informed his parents that he was resigning. Al's parents were distressed, but they accepted his decision that he would not be happy as a naval officer. They told him, however, that the decision was his and that he would have to take the consequences of it. Since Al resigned in midyear, he had to serve time as an enlisted man before being released from the navy. This was very difficult for Al, and his lot was not made easier by the fact that his peers knew he was a dropout from the Academy. But from this experience, Al learned a lot about what position he desired in life, difficult though the learning was. And the fact that his parents stood back and let him take the consequences of a decision they disagreed with was more useful to Al in straightening out his aspirations than any other action they could have taken.

By knowing when to assist and when to back off, Al's parents furthered the process of enabling Al to work out his own status goals and to develop strategies to accomplish them. His parents have the satisfaction of seeing Al gradually moving from NQA to adult.

Emotional Support

Young children rely on their parents to keep them feeling good about themselves. When they cut or bruise themselves, they go to Mom or Dad to fix the hurt. When they are snubbed by friends, they go to their parents to be comforted. As adolescents, they talk to their parents about how they feel about school or part-time jobs, about which member of the opposite sex they like at that particular time of the day, and on and on. When a date goes well, they show off in front of their parents. When it goes badly, they go to their parents to ease the sense of tragedy and to help the adjustment to what they feel will be a certain future as a social outcast.

The childhood period is one where support is sought and admonitions are usually followed. The adolescent period is one where advice is sought, but interpretations, support, and admonitions given by the parents are often challenged, and many times ignored. The relationship between parents and children of these ages, nevertheless, is a mutually active one. By contrast, parents can assist their children best through the NQA period by assuming a less active role. They should encourage their NQA's to work their feelings out as well as they can themselves by talking with their peers or with other adults with whom they have a relationship.

The NQA period is the time when young people are establishing their own home away from their parents—achieving their emotional independence. NQA's are looking for others, beside their parents, who will be significant in their lives, and most of all they are looking for one person whom they can count on for emotional support.

Parents sometimes find it difficult to give up their roles as chief providers of emotional support. They enjoy feeling that they are still the most important part of their children's reference group. When parents are the ones to whom the NQA unfailingly turns, the parents always know just what is going on and have input into the decisions made by the NQA. Thus, the parents can retain a large measure of control over what the NQA does, a control that sooner or later the NQA will come to resent.

This does not mean that parents should ignore the emotional needs of the NQA or turn a cold shoulder to pleas for help. For instance, parents should permit the occasional collect call when the away-from-home NQA becomes upset and must talk to someone who understands. This usually results in an outpouring that continues until parents remind the NQA that his or her troubles are costing them money. The expensive monologue should be taken by parents as the NQA's way of sorting out feelings about a difficult situation. Any input that the parents may have should be directed toward helping NQA's to see the situation realistically, to evaluating its seriousness as rationally as possible, and then to suggest, never to order, a variety of solutions. The inclination to cradle the NQA's symbolically, as parents used to do physically, must be avoided.

NQA's should not depend too heavily on parents for emotional support, for this will hamper their ability to form mature relationships. Parents should not demand that NQA's come to them at the first sign of emotional difficulties. Here, as in the other areas, a separation must take place. Parents have to let go. NQA's must get free.

It is important for parents of NQA's to realize the extent of their influence over their sons and daughters. Some parents use this influence to try to control their NQA's as long as they can, even though this eventually results in either a complete breakdown in the relationship or an overly dependent NQA who is unable to break away at all. Other parents use their influence to help NQA's to become free, to assure their steady movement toward adulthood. This is the appropriate use of parental authority. . . to use it so that by its use the need for it gradually will cease to exist.

REFERENCES

[1]B. Mandel, ed., *Welfare in America*, Englewood Cliffs, N.J.: Prentice-Hall Inc., 1975, pp. 112–16.

[2]T. Gordon, *P. E. T. Inc.*, *Parent Effectiveness Training* (New York: New American Library, 1975).

FOR ADDITIONAL READING

Ashcraft, N., and A. Scheflen, *People Space*. New York: Anchor Books, 1976.

An in-depth discussion of the private domain with which people surround themselves.

Halpern, H., *Cutting Loose*. New York: Simon & Schuster, 1976.

How to change old ways of relating to parents and replace them with relationships based on respect for each other's separateness.

Smith, M., *When I Say No, I Feel Guilty*. New York: Bantam Books, 1975.

Discusses the differences between assertiveness and manipulation. Gives suggestions on how to avoid being pushed around by other people.

3

Money
and
Finances

It is frequently said that everybody talks about the weather, but nobody does anything about it. Money and finances are the exact opposite. Everybody is doing something about them all the time, but nobody talks much. According to psychiatrist James A. Knight,[1] a discussion of income and outgo is nearly as taboo today as a discussion of sex was during the Victorian period. Guilt and hidden meanings abound. The NQA spouts pop jargon about the sins of materialism. Parents speak vaguely of potential disasters inherent in wasting money, of spending "too much." But nobody ever explains what is "too much" or why.

Money probably isn't as much fun to talk about as sex, but it should be discussed openly because many of the issues that families face as the NQA struggles for independence revolve around the use of family resources.

It may be difficult for some parents to tell if their NQA is still emotionally or psychologically dependent, but nobody should have any problem spotting financial dependency. This is not an abstract concept. It the parents give any money at all or provide any kind of support at all, then financial dependence still exists. Christmas or birthday gifts don't count unless they are given in such a fashion that the young person grows to rely on them for regular maintenance. Financial dependency exists when a parent gives, and an NQA accepts, any help for the NQA's basic support. The degree of dependency varies widely. It can range all the way from those who are completely supported by parents to those who need only minimal help.

Some of those who are most dependent have made unsuccessful attempts at breaking away. Included in this group are NQA's who started college but came home before midterms or those who tried sharing an apartment but gave it up after a few quarrels with roommates. These NQA's might be employed full time, but their hourly wage is low, and what they earn they spend on themselves almost as though their salary were an allowance. This complete dependency is one extreme.

At the other end of the spectrum is the NQA who is a college student with an excellent grant and a part-time campus job. This person might be self-supporting nine months of the year, but he or she still plans to live at home during the summer months while working in a nearby factory to earn the money needed during the next school year.

Some NQA's, after seeming to achieve financial independence, fall upon what they consider to be "hard times." They return home and expect parents to reassume the burden of their support. Usually they are unemployed for any one of a variety of reasons. Some have been fired from jobs because of irresponsibility. Some have been laid off because of a recession. There are those who have graduated from college or a job training program but cannot find work in their field. Perhaps the returned NQA is a young mother who has decided to get a divorce, or it might be that the NQA dropped out a while back to join the counterculture or a religious group and now wants to be back in the mainstream. Some are recuperating from an illness, perhaps hepatitis or mononucleosis, which are quite common in this group. Perhaps the NQA has just quit a much hated job and is seeking a new career direction. The young man recently discharged from the navy fits into this category of returnee.

All these examples have one thing in common. If NQA's

assume complete financial responsibility for themselves, their standard of living will drop. On the other hand, when parents assume part or all of the burden of support for NQA's, the parents' standard of living is lowered. This tug of war causes many of the problems between parents and NQA's, but other conflicts also exist.

NQA's know as well or better than their parents that they are no longer children. Perhaps their parents would not agree, but NQA's feel that they are capable and ready to enjoy maximum freedom. They want to be allowed to choose their own friends, food, clothing, work, political ideology, ethics, methods of worship or meditation, their own goals, and their own measurements for standards of achievement. They demand the opportunity to be themselves in all ways. On the other hand, worrying about money, spending time to acquire it, figuring how to spend it wisely, and planning for the future can be seen as a limitation of one's personal freedom. Indeed it is! This is, unfortunately or not, a limitation with which adults have to learn to live. Parents have the unwelcome task of teaching NQA's that to have freedom, they must be willing to accept responsibility for themselves—their finances as well as their actions. They must learn that no one is truly free "to be me" as long as another person holds the financial reins. It is the task of the parents to encourage NQA's to desire financial independence and to help them to recognize that all other freedoms are illusory until that is achieved.

To do this, and maintain a good relationship, is a challenge that parents must accept, but all too often parents reject the challenge and try instead to use their financial resources to control their children. They may make loud complaints to anyone who will listen, but it is obvious that many parents really get a lot of satisfaction out of their NQA's continued dependence. The NQA's do a lot of complaining too. They want to have freedom without taking any responsibility; the parents want them to take responsibility without giving them any freedom.

NQA's are often quite unrealistic about their parents' income. They are like a three-year-old who sees the father as a giant even though he may be somewhat less than average in height. All that matters to the three-year-old is that his or her father is a lot bigger. NQA's have the same kind of shortsightedness about their parents' income.

Parents almost always earn more than NQA's; therefore they seem rich by comparison. This is usually complicated by the NQA's lack of information about the family income or budget. Lots of parents would find it easier to tell an NQA that he or she was conceived before the wedding than they would to disclose the exact amount of Mom's and Dad's income or the size of the mortgage.

Parents and NQA's both find it difficult to be realistic about the NQA's income. On one hand, we are told by the media that the highest rate of unemployment is found in this age group. On the other hand, when NQA's are working, even at the minimum wage, they may be earning enough to provide themselves with a standard of living that the parents enjoyed 25 years ago when they first assumed responsibility for themselves. Many NQA's earn far more than the minimum wage. Still, it is not always enough to pay for the many material comforts that Americans now regard as necessary. Thus, you find the NQA who is living at home for free until he or she finishes paying for a stereo or a car.

The age of affluence and the era of the child-centered home combine with the lengthening period of financial dependency to produce stress in the American family. Finances can be both a problem and an answer.

Who Owns the Washing Machine?

It is a generally accepted rule in our society that parents will support their children through high school. This support includes food, shelter, clothing, and medical care, and often transportation and an allowance. There may be arguments about how much of the parents' income young people can claim, but there is no doubt that parents have the responsibility and children have the rights. The laws of all 50 states enforce this cultural attitude.

A typical statute reads:

> . . .the father of a minor child is criminally liable for his support and in the event of his failure its mother becomes so liable. . . If the parent neglects to provide articles necessary for his child under his charge, according to his circumstances, a third person may in good faith supply such necessaries and recover reasonable value from the parents.[2]

Some state laws entitle the parents to "earnings or services" of the minor, but more state laws concern themselves with protecting the minor with a large income (a movie star, for example) from being exploited by the parents.

This is not to say that young people through high school age have had no experience with money. On the contrary, a great deal of money passes through their hands. According to a Rand Corporation poll, teen-agers between the ages of 13–19 spent $25.3 billion in 1974, a recession year.[3]

In that year, approximately 30 million young persons were in this age bracket, and the average spent by each was about $840.00. Girls outspent the boys by about 10%. The older persons in this age bracket were likely to have spent more money than the younger ones. Some of the money spent was money they earned themselves.

Young people often begin earning money at an early age; first, perhaps, by selling lemonade, later by baby-sitting, selling newspapers, even later by ushering in theaters, waiting on or busing tables, frying hamburgers, or staffing summer playgrounds. They work on and off. Perhaps they will be on full time in the summer, part time in the winter, quit for three months to go out for football or for six weeks to take part in a play. Most of the jobs these young people get are menial and pay the minimum wage allowed.

The jobs require little training or responsibility. And, except in some depressed areas, or large cities, young persons in this age bracket who really try can find some sort of employment. They can afford to work for a low wage since they are not self-supporting.

Almost always, the money that these young persons earn is spent on themselves, for extras above and beyond what are considered to be the parents' duty, although this may relieve parents of a portion of the support burden. It can be of considerable help if adolescents provide their own spending money, augment the clothing allowance, or even save for college. However, it is rare for high schoolers to pay room and board, or contribute in any other way to their basic support. Probably very few in middle-class homes volunteer to contribute their earnings to help pay the mortgage or the electric or water bills.

Then, a day arrives when these young persons graduate from high school. Most of them are, or will soon turn, 18. In 75% of the states, these young persons newly 18 are also legally adults. In three states, legal majority is reached at age 19. In a number of the rest, which still retain majority at age 21, legislation is pending to reduce the legal age. By federal statute, all persons 18 years and older can vote and be drafted.

At the age of majority, these young persons also can leave home, marry without parental permission, obtain a loan in their own name, and go to an adult jail. Parents are no longer legally required to provide "maintenance, protection, and education." The adolescent has become an NQA. [4]

When young persons reach the age of majority, parents begin to have a change in attitude as they see their responsibilities toward these children coming to an end. One mother expressed it this way: "I stopped asking her what she was planning to do and started asking her when she intended to start."

For NQA's, this can be a period of confusion and resentment. All of a sudden, it seems to them, they are expected to bridge the enormous gulf between spending their income on extras above and beyond their basic support and producing an income that will be the major factor in determining their standard of living.

The realization by NQA's that they alone are going to have to assume the burden of their own financial responsibility or irresponsibility comes slowly to some and overnight to others. But common to all NQA's is the dawning recognition that sooner or later they will be moving away from home; and the washing machine, the television, and everything else called the "comforts of home" will stay behind.

How Much Is More or Less?

The rising cost of living and the rising level of expectations of middle-class America cause great problems in communications between parents and NQA's. If there really is a generation gap, it is probably to be found in this area. There has been such rapid change in the past few years that parents and their children have very different ideas about ways of spending money and the value of the dollars being spent.

Everyone knows what inflation is. The problem with inflation is not in the definition of it, but that NQA's got into the act at a later date than their parents, so they have different reactions. They don't remember a time when this, that, and the other thing was half the price, even though that time was just a few short years ago, because they were not buying this, that, and the other thing at the time. Talking about a time when hamburger was three pounds for $1.00 is as relevant to an NQA as talking of a time when a chicken cost 10 cents is to the parents. NQA's are inclined to think that whatever the current price of gasoline, it is fair enough. Up a bit perhaps, but not excessive. They simply can't imagine that anyone would still be alive today who could remember gasoline at five gallons for $1.00.

Rising expectations is a catchall term for those things once thought to be luxuries that have now become necessities. Some of our present-day needs were not even invented 20 years ago. Mother was not concerned if she didn't own a frost-free refrigerator in her first years of marriage—there weren't any. The parent who owned a car at the age of 20 knew that not everyone was so lucky. Today, a twenty-year-old who doesn't own a car—and there are many who don't—feels deprived. Color television came on the market in 1954, but it did not become popular until about 10 years later. According to the U.S. Census Bureau report of 1974, 67% of American homes owned a color television set in 1973.[5] In less than 20 years, this unheard-of luxury had become almost standard equipment.

The rising level of expectations includes more than possessions. A federally financed study by the National Assessment of Educational Progress, a project of the Education Commission of the United States, found that 44% of American 17-year-olds were hoping for professional careers.[6] Consider also the higher and higher salaries that we are told are necessary to keep up with inflation. The minimum wage is over $2.50 an hour, which means that a working NQA is going to earn at least $80.00 a week. Parents remember a time when the same kinds of work paid 30 or maybe 40 cents an hour, and people were glad to get it. It really comes as a shock for parents to hear an unemployed NQA say in disgust, "I can't take that job. It only pays $700.00 a month. You can't expect me to work for that kind of money." It is particularly shocking when the NQA is sitting in the parents' living room with his or her feet on the parents' coffee table, watching the parents' TV, and drinking the parents' beer.

One young woman recently received a research assistantship from the university she attends. It pays $4,800.00 per year for 20 hours per week, while she studies for her master's degree. When she expressed concern that she would be unable to live on that amount of money, her parents could not muster much sympathy for her plight. After receiving his Ph.D. in 1953, her father received $4,400.00 as his first salary, and with that he supported a wife and two children. "But money was worth more then," says the daughter. "Not that much more" was the reply. But she finds it as difficult to see from her parents' perspective as they do from hers.

Another example is the following scene, which has been played in most homes, although the prices or the item discussed may vary.

An NQA walks in the door with a pair of shoes that look like sneakers, leather bound, quite fancy. "Look what I got," he says, "and, wow, they were only $24.50!" "You've got to be kidding!" replies the parent, whose astonishment is equal to the NQA's, but with quite a different reason. The NQA is pleased at the wonderful buy he got, since the normal price is $28.90 and this was the last pair left in his size at the sale price. Furthermore, he *has* to have them because everybody is wearing this kind of shoe and they are very comfortable. The parent is remembering a time when sneakers cost about $3.00, and poor people always wore them because that was all they could afford. Parents are constantly amazed at the cost or necessity of an item that NQA's take for granted.

At the same time, many parents show concern at NQA's inability to earn enough money to provide these so-called necessities of life for themselves. Parents talk a lot about their "poor kids."

The "poor kids" have to live at home because they cannot afford the present high rents. Naturally, the "poor kids" wear grubby clothes. They can't afford the price of good ones. The "poor kid's" car has died, and somebody has to drive him or her to work. Repair costs are so high these days. The "poor kids" didn't want to take any money out of the savings account for any of these things, for heaven's sake. That's for college next year or to furnish the apartment or go on a trip.

The same parents are, on the one hand, angry because NQA's have no appreciation for the value of money, and, on the other hand, are worrying about the "suffering" their "poor kids" experience because the rising cost of living makes it impossible instantly to own or do everything that the rising level of expectations makes necessary.

NQA's are as confused as their parents. They hear their parents complain that the electric bill has gone up. "By how much?" the NQA asks. "Oh," replies the parent, "I guess it will put our bill up another couple of dollars a month this time. We are really going to have to remember to turn off the lights now." The NQA is completely mystified. He or she knows that Dad's salary is higher this year, that he just got a good raise. How can the parents be so concerned over a mere $24.00 more?

It is difficult to explain to a young person who has not yet felt the real pressure of inflation that it is not just this year's increase in the cost of electricity that bothers parents. It is that combined with the increased cost of water, taxes, telephone, mortgage payments, and food and clothing added to the price hike of last year and the year before. NQA's may have read somewhere that, although the average salary of wage earners has increased in the last 10 years, their spending power has decreased. But these are only words to an NQA. They may have seen things they are interested in go up in price, like records, but they cannot fully understand the anger and fear that parents feel as they see the position they have labored so hard to achieve being eaten away by events so completely out of their control.

There is no easy solution to all of this. But recognizing the reason why some of the problems in communications arise is the beginning of a solution. When the NQA buys an item that the parents have not purchased in many years, which now costs three times what the parents think it should cost, they shouldn't direct their anger at the NQA. The rise in price is not the fault of the young person. On the other hand, parents should recognize that what an NQA wants, or even what parents want for an NQA, may not be as necessary as it first appears. For parents to buffer the "poor kids" from economic reality and then to turn around and complain that the "darn kids" don't know the value of a dollar is inconsistent. It contributes nothing toward helping an NQA to get free from financial dependency.

More about Great Expectations

As children grow from infancy to adulthood, their needs and wants grow along with them. The six-year-old with a burning desire to own a fancy bicycle with a banana seat, or a GI Joe doll with some of the equipment, is likely to be given such delights for Christmas or on a birthday. Such expenditures do not affect the family's standard of living. Parents can still purchase a new washing machine if one is needed.

But NQA's are no longer satisfied with toys or bicycles. They want expensive ski equipment, stereos, a college education, and automobiles, things of such great cost that the purchase might be made only with real sacrifice on the parents' part. When parents choose not to make such a purchase,—say for a car for the NQA—they tend to feel guilty if they go car shopping on their own. It can be even more guilt-producing for parents to tell the NQA that they have spent their limit for this year on the NQA's education, when they are at the same moment packing to go on a long-planned and expensive vacation. It is easier to deal with the NQA's who get angry and tell their parents that they have no right to spend money so foolishly on themselves than those who affect patient suffering. They sigh so piteously.

"Well," they say, "I suppose you would really want to do that before you get too old. I can always work an extra 20 hours a week while you are enjoying yourself in Florida" or wherever anyone was going. The "old folks" may have it firmly fixed in their minds that they will not allow the NQA to control the family spending, and still they find it is difficult not to rise to this bait.

Some friends provide an example. Their 10-year-old portable TV set had had it. After careful comparison shopping, they purchased a larger console model. When their son, who has had about the average amount of ups and downs in setting himself goals in life, came home on vacation, his parents expected him to enjoy this new purchase as much as they did. After all, he had frequently said that the only time he watched TV was when he was home. At school he was too busy.

They brought him to the family room. "Look," they said with pride, "isn't it gorgeous?"

He stared. His eyes narrowed. "It's a lot bigger than the last one, isn't it?" (Translation—"You spent a bundle.")

"Well, err, yes, it is a little bigger. Sure," they admitted.

"Humph," he said, "getting pretty fancy in your old age, aren't you?" (Translation—"I could have used that money, and you blew it on yourselves.")

All the comparisons between the son's life and their own ran through the parents' heads. Their nice home, his tacky apartment, and so on. Yet, they were supporting him rather well at college and were angry at the implication that what they were spending was not enough. This son had placed his parents on the defensive, but they did not want to get into the kind of discussion that begins, "Damn it, your father works very hard to keep you and your sister in college, and if he wants to relax a bit in front of a good TV set, he has every right to do so. . . ."

What to do?

The best response is the shortest. They smiled and said, "Maybe so," and changed the subject. There is no more reason for parents to justify a purchase to one of their children than there is for them to explain it to a next-door neighbor, who could probably also offer suggestions for other uses for that particular bit of money.

Some NQA's do not content themselves with criticizing their parents' expenditures. They go even further and take the attitude that "what's yours is mine, and what's ours is everybody's."

In the counterculture, materialism is a dirty word. Private ownership is frowned upon and to refuse to share is bad, bad, bad. In a true communal situation, this can be a positive and sound idea. That is in theory, of course, but in the "real world," materialism is often most clearly defined by those who want you to share something you own with them. NQA's, who tend to use the jargon of the counterculture, sometimes try this ethic to hold on to use of their parents' resources.

Suppose an NQA has plans to take a group of friends to hear a rock concert in a town 125 miles away. Mom's station wagon must be used to have enough room. Mom and Dad are not thrilled, but they have agreed. "Okay," says Dad, "but the tank was just filled, so please return it the same way." Now hear the howls of protest.

"This is a beautiful thing I am doing for my friends. We share everything, and we never worry about these materialistic details," says the NQA. "The trouble with your generation is that all you ever think about is money, money, money. If only you could see the joy of not feeling possessive about anything."

This kind of talk makes many child-centered parents feel guilty. They think their children are truly generous, forgetting how easy it is to be generous when you own very little yourself, when the things you are sharing were paid for by someone else.

On the other hand, parents cannot expect their NQA's who are living within their means to give reasons that the parents will find logical for every expenditure the NQA might make. NQA's get furious at the idea that anyone should tell them how to spend their money. "It's mine," they say. "I earned it." And they are right.

A separation of incomes must occur. NQA's incomes can be expected to rise. Parents are beginning to look forward to a leveling off of income as well as expenses, and eventually to retirement. Both NQA's and parents should learn to plan for a future that will exclude each financially.

Parents can teach their NQA's much about financial management, but there are many who don't even try. The reasons are as varied as the families.

Some don't realize how little the NQA's really know. "The kid should know about money," they say. "She's handled her own clothing allowance since she was 13." That's a good start, to be sure, but it's only a start.

Other parents can think of no way to get their points across. "Teach the kids to keep a checkbook—you must be kidding! The lousy schools don't even teach them how to add." Well, many people don't learn much about math until they see the need. NQA's have the need whether they know it or not, and parents can help them to recognize it.

There are many parents who would prefer to keep their sons and daughters in economic ignorance so that they can continue to use their financial superiority to control the behavior of NQA's. This losing proposition is related to the struggle for power and authority.

Some NQA's are cut off from this educative process because of sex differences; many parents still see financial responsibility differently for their sons than for their daughters. Today's society dictates the need for both sexes to learn the skills that will make it possible to become competent financial managers.

Most young women today intend to get married and have children. It may seem that they share the same goal as did their mothers and grandmothers—but there are real differences. Most women used to get married because "that's what you did." The only financial skill necessary was to learn how to get by on the husband's income, and the trick was "to catch" a "good provider" who would joyfully take over where the family left off. Young women were sometimes sent to teachers' colleges, into nurses' training, or taught to type because it was important to have "something to fall back on." But "falling back" was strictly an emergency measure until another "good provider" came to the rescue. A wise woman who "played her cards right" could remain financially *dependent* throughout her entire life. This was the principal goal.

Even in the "good old days," however, this was both romantic perhaps and certainly unrealistic. In actual fact, many women found it necessary to support themselves, their children, and sometimes even their husbands in jobs ranging from college professor to sweatshop laborer. But no matter how many women were working, it was considered deviant behavior. Prejudice was so great against financially responsible women that only recently have women been able to get free of financial subservience to their husbands, a subservience that was not affected by the size of the woman's income or the amount of property she had brought to the marriage. Only in the last few years have legal battles been won that make it possible for women to obtain credit cards, mortgages, and many other types of loans in their own names.

Today, young women may still plan to marry and have a child or two, but most expect to work until they get married, continue working until the first child is born, and often as not keep on working. Those who leave the labor force while their children are young often return to work when the youngest is in school. Marriage is gradually becoming more a partnership of equals. Income is pooled, financial decisions are shared, and the principal goals of marriage are love and companionship.

The popular press is now full of advice to women on how to prepare themselves to handle their own financial affairs

during extended periods in an unmarried state, whether because they have remained single, or are divorced or widowed.
Almost one-fourth of all households are headed by single women. Since the late 1960s, the number of households headed
by women has risen by 46%. The U.S. Census Bureau says,
furthermore, that there are now nearly 13 million once-
married women 35 or older. Of women now married, three out
of four will spend an average of 18 years as widows. Half of
those will be widows by the age of 56.[7]

Some parents are uncomfortable with the changing
status of women. Many of their daughters are in agreement;
not all are feminists. However, parents should understand
that, feminist or not, daughters are under pressure to learn
financial skills. Parents have to be ready to deal with the
worries and fears that female NQA's may have regarding
their ability to provide a desired standard of living for themselves, as well as for their children. These are the same kinds
of worries with which the male NQA always has had to cope.
Daughters need as much training in financial management as
the sons.

Some parents are reluctant to teach the financial facts of
life to their NQA's for the same reason that they did not teach
the sexual facts of life earlier. An attitude exists that "nice
people just don't talk about things like that."

Parental ignorance may be offered as an excuse. Parents
often do not realize the amount of financial skill they have
accumulated over the years. Knowledge, like income and size,
is relative. Father may feel that he knows very little about
the Internal Revenue Service, but he has been turning in his
tax returns for the last 20 or so years. In fact, he knows a
great deal.

Mother may get very coy about her "feminine" inability
to balance a checkbook, but she must have evolved some sort
of system. (Maybe now is a good time to learn a better one.)
Both parents have probably handled charge accounts, bills,
rents or mortgage payments, insurance, loans, savings or in-

vestments, and all the things that are part of the family's financial structure. Parents have vast stores of information to impart if they compare themselves with NQA's instead of comparing themselves with the CPA who lives next door.

So, we have defined NQA's in financial terms, given some reasons why problems arise, and suggested that parents can teach the economic facts of life to their NQA's.

But what of the reader who says, "That's all very well for you to say . . . only how do you teach these things and what are you supposed to teach anyway?" And what of the NQA who says, "What do we need to know?"

Good questions! Let's try to answer them in the next chapter.

REFERENCES

[1]J.A. Knight, *For the Love of Money*. Philadelphia: J.B. Lippincott Co., 1968.

[2]*Martindale-Hubbell Law Directory*, 106th annual ed. (Summit, N.J.: Martindale-Hubbell, 1974).

[3]*The Milwaukee Journal*, December 5, 1975.

[4]*Martindale-Hubbell Law Directory*.

[5]*1977–The U.S. Fact Book*, from the Statistical Abstract of the United States as prepared by the Bureau of Census, Dept. of Commerce, 97th Ed. (New York: Grossett & Dunlap, 1977).

[6]*The National Observer*, November 20, 1976.

[7]*The National Observer*, November 13, 1976.

The
Financial
Facts
of
Life

To become financially responsible adults, NQA's need to understand how and why the family makes its financial decisions. This involves discussion of the family income and expenditures. Either parents or NQA's can begin the process.

Sharing Financial Information

NQA's who ask tactful questions that show they are genuinely interested will probably find their parents happy to share their concerns. On the other hand, when a young person says without warning, "Say, Dad (or Mom), how much bread do you drag in?", Dad (or Mom) is likely to answer, "None of your business!" The NQA who asks a series of questions about the expenses of running the household will get better results.

How much does it cost each month for electricity? Heat? Water? Telephone? How does the billing work? Do you pay every month? What happens if you aren't home when the meter reader comes? What kind of taxes do we pay? How do they figure that? What rent do we pay? Has it gone up? What does it include? What are the mortgage payments each month? How long does that go on? Has the house gone up in value? Are repairs a major expense? How does inflation affect our family? Hey, Mom, how much does the family spend on food every month? NQA's who ask questions such as these, and then listen to the answers, show that they understand that everything in the home does cost something and must be paid for by someone.

Most parents will be happy that the young person is interested, and they will take that interest as a sign of maturity.

If the young person is not showing an interest, parents can initiate the exchange. Explain that the purpose is to help the NQA understand how the family reaches decisions about spending; it is not just a revelation of problems. Start by showing them the bills for various household expenses. Send them to the bank to make the mortgage payment. Show them the insurance policies and explain how they work and how much they cost. Talk about utility costs, food bills, clothing and recreation expenses. Tell them if major expenses for household repairs, the car, or whatever, are expected in the near future. Does the family have investments, retirement plans, IRA accounts, or savings? Do any of these earn money that is part of the family income? For single parents, how much child support do they receive? Is it regular? To what age will the other parent be paying? It should be explained to the NQA that some of the payments that parents make are purchasing benefits that the NQA's will eventually share because the size of their eventual inheritance will be increased or because the NQA will not have to assume the support of the parents when they get too old to work. NQA's should be made aware that the direct payments they receive are not the only benefits that parents provide for them. If the family is having financial difficulties, this information should be shared with the NQA.

Parents often find it very difficult to talk about their finances with their children. Some husbands don't even tell wives, and vice versa. It just is not part of American culture to talk openly about money. Very few people know the exact amount of any person's income except their own. For instance, at a party it is perfectly acceptable to ask where someone lives or works, how many children they have, how long they have lived in the area, what kind of car they drive, and many other questions that demand quite personal information. But *no one* at a party ever says, "How much money do you make?" "Is that all of it, or do you have investments too?" "Any hope that somebody will die off and leave you something?" "Do you still get alimony?" People simply do not ask such questions, although they are not really more personal than others that are frequently asked. This reluctance is carried over into our families.

There are other reasons why parents find it difficult to talk about their income. Some parents have, over the years, given their NQA's the impression that the family income is far larger than it is. Others have suffered financial setbacks. They may find it embarrassing to reveal the truth in either case. Not to do so, however, is asking for trouble since the NQA's think such parents are tightwads, even when they are committing a disproportionately large share of the family income to the NQA.

Some parents fear that if the NQA learns how large their income really is, their demands will increase. Indeed, an increase in demands is a probable result if the young person is told *only* the income. The outgo also must be discussed to provide a balance.

Parents who have debts that are bothering them are often reluctant to talk about them. Too often, all the NQA's hear is the "don't." "Don't go into debt." "Don't charge that." "Don't borrow too much." The parents are too embarrassed to tell NQA's that their fears and admonitions are prompted by their own bad experiences or foolishness. "What," say the parents, "will they think of us? We never would have charged those expensive new drapes and the carpeting if we had known how much Sara was going to need this year at school."

Maybe not, but the money *has* been spent and the parents *must* pay off their debts. That teaches the NQA's to do so too. Frankness helps the NQA's to begin to think of their parents as knowledgeable human beings, not just authority figures who pretend perfection.

Some parents don't want their NQA's to see how much they have committed themselves to spend on something in which the whole family does not share; they feel guilty about money they spend for their own pleasure. Membership at the yacht or country club was great as long as the NQA was participating too, but now he or she wants to go to an expensive college and a choice has to be made—the parents cannot afford both. This question eventually will be settled on grounds that include more than the financial aspects. Do parents really care about the club? Is this Dad's (or Mom's) only outlet, one that makes it possible for him (or her) to function the rest of the time in a competitive job that long ago ceased to provide much pleasure? Or was the membership kept because the NQA enjoyed the activity? What are the NQA's reasons for wanting to go to the expensive college? Do the parents agree that the NQA's reasons are sound? In the meantime, it won't hurt anybody for the NQA to know how much a membership costs or the expenses involved in any type of recreational activity.

NQA's are usually amazed to find out how much money is committed every month and how little of what had seemed to be an enormous income is left over. Sometimes NQA's even discover that their own paychecks give them more money to spend as they choose than their parents have. A jolting realization!

Parents should not expect that the NQA will learn everything there is to know about the family's finances in one marathon family conference, although that might be a way to start. It will take time for the NQA to begin to appreciate the many facets of the parents' financial problems and management. After all, parents have been at it for 20 or so years.

They can't expect the NQA to learn it all in a couple of hours. But parents can resolve to take the NQA into their confidence and share their knowledge. That decision eventually will pay off with good results. The first is that the NQA's will base their expectations for financial support on a realistic appraisal of the family's resources. Second, the NQA's will gain knowledge that will make it possible for them eventually to be independent. There are also possibilities of two other side benefits. Often the NQA's come up with suggestions for handling financial problems that the parents have not thought of. Another is that, in organizing themselves to present information to the NQA, parents may discover new ways to handle their finances.

Good teachers often say that they learn more from their students than they teach. This is as true for parents and NQA's as it is in any other learning situation.

Checking Accounts—What's in a Name?

At the same time that the NQA is learning about the family's finances, he or she also should be gaining experience with banking. An NQA who is reluctant to open a checking account should be encouraged to do so. Often NQA's do not see the importance of having a checking account in his or her own name. "I don't have enough money to make it worth the bother," NQA's explain. To them, a checkbook is only a convenient way to pay bills, and they have few bills to pay.

Financially immature people cash paychecks and keep the money in a drawer. If money must be sent somewhere by mail, they try to get someone else to write a check in return for the cash. When they lose track of money, they assume it has been lost or stolen, even though this may not be the case. One who keeps money in a drawer usually does not have an accurate idea of how much money is there.

Checking accounts solve many of these problems, but they offer more than just a better way to keep track of money. They make it easier for people to learn an idea that is basic to proper financial management—*Money is more than cash!* People, including NQA's and misers, who keep cash in dresser drawers or in socks under the mattress or even in piggy banks with a key, see money as a real, physical entity. They do not see that a dollar bill is just a piece of paper and a quarter is a slice of silver-coated plastic, which in themselves are worth nothing. They cannot be eaten, worn, or used to keep warm. A dollar bill is a contract between the holder and the U.S. government. The government states that it guarantees to the holder that there is, in the government's possession, an equivalent value in gold or silver, which cannot be eaten, worn, or used to keep warm either. This guarantee tells the holder that he or she can purchase goods amounting in value to whatever one dollar's worth of gold might be worth at the moment of purchase. It is, after all, a symbol like a poker chip. The difference is that its value is established by the government rather than by a group of people sitting around a card table.

Jean Piaget, the famous Swiss psychologist, demonstrated that young children do not have the mental ability to think abstractly.[1] Only at the beginning of adolescence, at 12 or 13 years, do children begin to develop the cognitive powers that enable them to tell the difference between reality and possibility; that is, to think abstractly. They become able to see money as a concept, which can change in value and form, not just as a thing with only one kind of physical reality.

Adults seldom examine the thought processes that go into making these abstractions; so here it would be a good idea for parents to stop to think for a moment. Many never see or handle their paychecks at all; they may go directly from the employer to the bank. Others see them briefly as they make the transfer themselves. In either event, there is a chunk one never sees since the government has already taken its share in social security and income taxes. After it is deposited, some of the money may go into a savings account, some bills may be paid, property taxes or insurance money is sometimes held aside in an escrow account. Other bills are paid by personal check. For travel, one purchases travelers' checks or uses credit cards. All of this is routine and is accomplished without much thought because the use of symbols other than cash for purchase and payment has become automatic. In spite of this, few parents recognize the amount of learning and practice they have had that gives them the ability to use symbols as they do.

Adults may handle large sums of money but usually only small amounts of cash. NQA's, who generally deal with much smaller amounts of money, frequently handle much larger amounts of cash. They are capable of dealing with abstractions, but they have not yet felt the necessity or had the education to do so. Parents can provide some of each.

By insisting that NQA's acquire and use a checking account, parents provide an important part of the NQA's education in the modern use of money. First, the young person is taught to avoid the immature financial policy of "When you got it, you spend it! When you don't got it, you don't!" A checking account makes it easier to plan for future expenditures, and it provides a record of where the money went. More important, a checking account teaches NQA's that the use of actual cash plays a minor function in the present economic system.

NQA's learn this by the experience of seeing a deposit slip as money that they own and can spend by using a check—two new abstract symbols. The even more abstract symbol that comes to stand in place of hard cash is the NQA's signature on a check and, later on, on sales slips or contracts that authorize purchase and obligate payment from future earnings. The most difficult symbol of all to use without getting into trouble is the small plastic card that validates one's signature—the credit card. One's name written on the dotted line on a charge account slip is the most sophisticated symbol, for it goes far beyond what cash can do. Cash represents only the purchasing power a person has at the moment; credit and credit cards represent not only present purchasing power, but they also predict that the person's earning ability will exist into the future. Lack of concern for the future, a characteristic of young persons, makes the use of credit difficult to learn. Those who manage to obtain credit before they have had the experience of using a personal checking account are suffering a real disadvantage. In physical terms, it is like trying to learn to walk before learning to crawl.

Without doubt, parents should prod any reluctant NQA's into opening a checking account. Sometimes it is necessary to take them to the bank and make a small initial deposit. The account should be in the NQA's name. It should not be a joint account with the parents. This gives parents a way to begin the NQA's education for financial responsibility. Parents who are making funds available to the NQA can deposit them in the NQA's account. This will guarantee some use of it since the NQA will have to write a check to use the money.

If, after the account is opened, the young person comes crying that cash money has been lost or stolen, the parents may want to cry too, but they should curb the urge to be overly sympathetic. Something on the order of, "Oh, dear! What a shame! Too bad the money wasn't deposited in the bank where it would have been safe!" is both educational and sympathetic (even though the NQA might not think so at first). It isn't easy to be both at the same time, but it's a good idea to try.

Somebody has to teach the NQA how to balance a checkbook. If parents do not feel competent to do this, most banks will provide a teacher. NQA's also need to know that overdrafts cost money and that checks can clear in less than 24 hours. One can't write a check today on the strength of a deposit planned for next Tuesday.

Parents are not helping NQA's to learn financial responsibility when they cover overdrafts for them. It is important for young people to learn how to work their own way out of this kind of a jam. Most overdrafts result from small differences in the size of the check and the amount of the current balance. For example, perhaps an NQA has written a check for $60.00. It bounces because the balance in the bank is only $50. Parents often say, "Well, everybody makes a mistake once in a while. Let's just give the kid the $10.00. It's only a small amount, and it will save us all the embarrassment and the hassle." This is usually accompanied with asides about how the schools "don't teach them to do arithmetic any more."

This action is an error for many reasons. First, it is the NQA who should be embarrassed, not the parents. The NQA made the mistake and should take care of the hassle if any results.

A likely reason that the check has bounced is that the NQA forgot to deposit some money that is still in the dresser drawer, purse, or billfold. When parents rush to cover the bounced check, the undeposited money remains undeposited, and the bouncing checks will continue to appear until the young person is required to solve the problem that he or she has created.

There are other possible solutions to explore. The NQA may find it helpful to talk to someone at the bank. Perhaps an arrangement can be made if the NQA is going to be able to cover the overdraft in a few days. It may be necessary to contact the party to whom the check was written so that they will be aware that payment is forthcoming.

There is no need for parents to be cold and unfeeling. Their own previous experiences with "rubber" checks should help them to know how to be understanding. Parents can help their NQA's to look through their records to see if the problem is caused by a mistake in accounting. They can say things like "How embarrassing!" or "We certainly understand how this can happen." Parents can be loving and helpful in many ways without "bailing the kid out." But parents who are truly caring will not deprive their NQA's of the opportunity to learn ways to work themselves out of financial difficulties.

Debts—Paying the Piper

People who have attained legal majority can open charge accounts and obtain credit cards, and they are not required to tell their parents. Yet, parents often become quite frantic when NQA's run up debts.

Dunning letters arrive. "We are turning this case over to our lawyers." Sometimes there are threatening phone calls. It can be frightening, embarrassing, and irritating for the whole family, but it must be handled by the NQA. The person who has overspent must learn that sure and certain consequences will follow. He or she needs to experience the methods of debt collectors and to learn how to work out of such a mess.

The trouble is that parents tend to overidentify themselves with their NQA's; thus, the NQA's problems become the problems of the parents. It is easy to get panicky over debts, but the credit agencies didn't ask the parent's opinion as to whether John or Sue was capable of handling credit. Just the same, when problems arise, parents don't usually say, "John (or Sue) has a problem" or "The store has a problem." They say, "We have a problem," and they rush in to solve it.

NQA's are capable of solving their own problems, and parents who encourage them to do so are often amazed at their ability and ingenuity. It may not be easy, and the NQA's will need guidance from their parents. The NQA will probably have to give up a present or future pleasure for something enjoyed in the past. Perhaps it will be possible to return some merchandise, or take a second job if he or she can find one. Seeing the credit manager might help in working out an arrangement for payment. Legal advice may be necessary.

Some of the methods used by debt collectors are illegal. Many consumer protection laws have been enacted that are supposed to cut down on the harrassment, but often the persons they are supposed to protect are not aware that they exist.

In extreme cases, the NQA may have to declare bankruptcy. This is not the tragedy that it might at first seem. Although it is important to build up a good credit rating, and declaring bankruptcy does not help in achieving that goal, an NQA will experience less long-term effect than an older person does because people tend to say that the 20-year-old who has declared bankruptcy has learned a lesson and probably won't do that again. There are advantages to being an NQA, and the opportunity to make mistakes and not be permanently scarred is one of the most important.

Loans—Can You a Borrower or a Lender Be?

Good relationships between parents and NQA's are often hurt because the parents have loaned money to the NQA, and the money has not been repaid. This can happen because the meaning of the word "loan" is not the same to both parties. In many families, the distinction between "loans" and "gifts" is often quite fuzzy. Where do payments for ordinary, everyday support leave off, and loans begin? Why should people get confused about such a simple matter?

Parents may make financial support available to their NQA's in two ways. One is by outright gifts, which can range from complete support to a donation given at Christmas or on a birthday. A gift does not require any repayment, except perhaps a show of appreciation.

Another way in which parents may provide support is by allowing the NQA to borrow money from them. Unless there is a clear understanding that a "loan is a loan" regardless of how much support also may be provided in the form of gifts, misunderstandings, hurt feelings, and resentments will surely follow.

Here is a typical example. Sara is away at school. She has a part-time job, but her parents pay most of her school expenses.

The phone rings. "Mom, they are all fouled up at the financial aid office, and it turns out I'm not going to get paid until next month."

"Well, dear, why is that?"

"I don't know, Mom. It has something to do with when they get money from the government. I thought I'd get paid every month like I did last year, but this is from a different grant. I don't understand it, but anyway now I don't have the money to pay my share of the rent. Can you send me $60.00 please? I'll pay you back as soon as I get paid."

Mother sends the money, and several months pass. Sara makes no effort to repay. Finally, her parents decide to take action.

"Sara, you know you owe us $60.00. When are you going to pay? Didn't you get paid yet?"

"Gee, Mom and Dad, I guess I sort of forgot. Well, I'm still a little short because I bought those books I need for summer school, and I saved you a bundle because I had a chance to buy used books. Well, I guess I can spare $20.00. I'll give you some more next month. Say, Mom, can I take a couple of your jars of jam back to school? Everybody just loves it, and it's too expensive to buy. And, hey, I need some sheets. Can I take the old ones in the closet?

Was the $60.00 a loan or a gift? Was it basic support or something extra? Sara and her parents hold contradictory ideas about which is what and this has given rise to the hurt feelings which often precede conflict. Sara's parents feel they are being exploited. They see a loan that was not repaid—a sum of money spent which was above their original budget.

They feel hurt by what they define as Sara's irresponsible attitude. Sara will feel hurt if her parents insist that she pay back all of the $60.00. She thinks she has used the money well. After all, she spent it on something that her parents would have provided for her anyway.

This would be a good time for Sara and her parents to sit down and discuss the meaning of the word "loan." The parents should make it clear that, in order to keep their own accounts straight, they want all loans repaid as soon as possible, even if they must advance more at a later date. Sara is probably aware that by using the money for books ("Well, anyway, some of the money!") without telling her parents, she was too casual in her handling of the loan. She may not realize why this is important to her parents. Hopefully, they will see this not as a time to criticize Sara for her financial irresponsibility, but as an opportunity to teach her responsibility by explaining what they expect from her, and then holding firmly to that expectation.

Many parents provide financial assistance to their NQA's by making them a loan. That's fine, but the conditions of that type of assistance should be made clear. They should not be changed later if repayment becomes a chore for the NQA, or if the NQA decides he or she has another need for money, as Sara did with the books she bought. It later becomes very hard on young people when they discover to their horror that finance companies and banks are *never* confused about the meaning of the word "loan."

Other guidelines can minimize the possibility of "loan" conflict. First, parents must determine that the money the NQA has requested will be used well. Loans never should be made if parents think the purpose is frivolous. "Dad, Charlie and Mike are going skydiving on Saturday, and I want to go too. The thing is that the first jump costs $75.00. You have to have some lessons and learn how to fold your chute and all, and I won't have the money till my tax refund comes. Can I

borrow it from you?" "Sorry, son, when you get your own
money, you can spend it however you please. But skydiving
will have to wait till then."

Another example: "Mom, it's the cutest stuffed animal
I've ever seen. The thing is the sale only lasts till Saturday. If
you loan me the money, I'll pay you back just as soon as I get
a job this summer." "Sorry, dear!" This type of loan helps the
borrower achieve only a momentary pleasure; it should be
avoided like the plague.

If parents agree that the money the NQA has requested
will be used well, they still should not make a large loan until
the NQA has exhausted other possible sources of funding.
Send the NQA to a bank, the credit union, a finance company.
Have the NQA bring home information about rates of interest
and penalties for nonpayment. If one is able to obtain the loan
from another source, he or she should be encouraged to do so.
Sara probably could have arranged a short-term loan for her
rent from the same financial aid office that was holding up her
paycheck. If the young person finds that other sources of
funds are not available, the NQA will be much more apprecia-
tive of the service that the parents are providing.

Parents who have decided to make a loan can at the same
time teach the NQA that there is a cost involved in "renting
money." Interest should be charged, probably not as much as
the finance company would charge, but at least enough to
cover the interest that is lost because the money has been
removed from the parents' saving account.

Accurate records are important. Parents should have the
NQA sign a note. NQA's should demand receipts. There is no
quicker way to start an argument than for one person to say,
"You still owe me $20.00, and the other to reply, "No, I don't.
I paid that last week."

Caution should be exercised when cosigning a note with
anyone. Parents frequently cosign to make it possible for a
young person to buy a car, or for some other major purchase

that involves a large sum of money. Cosigning should *never* be done unless the young person has demonstrated reliability. If parents find themselves "holding the bag" because they have cosigned a note, they must be very careful not to make the same mistake a second time. Before further credit is extended, the NQA should be required to pay off the first note, plus any penalties that may have accrued.

It is best for everyone when NQA's obtain their loans from banks or credit unions without the involvement of parents. Obtaining and repaying a loan establishes a good credit rating. This will be useful later on when financing is needed on a scale that few parents can provide, perhaps to buy a house or begin a business.

In their day-to-day existence, NQA's have to learn to live within their incomes. Parents rarely should lend small amounts for pocket money. An important hallmark of adulthood is the ability to plan for the future. It is emphasized in folk sayings and stories. "You can't have your cake and eat it, too!" "If you burn your candle at both ends, it will not last the night!" Parents teach these lessons when they refuse to shell out five bucks, for example, so the NQA can go to the movies with the gang.

It is never wise for parents to hold a prized possession as collateral for a loan. Only a truly heartless parent could withhold a pair of skis on the weekend of the best snowfall of the season because John still owes $20.00. Parents who act as pawnbrokers find themselves stuck with high school class rings, tapes and records of last year's top recording groups, and a buildup of resentment that is difficult to overcome. Or else they say, "Oh, to heck with it," and give back whatever they were holding. Thus, they allow their NQA to continue thinking that loans and gifts are the same thing and, worse yet, that collaterals can be reclaimed at will.

The whole subject of loans must be approached with the knowledge that loaning money within a family is a risky business unless conditions are made clear and kept consistent. The parent–NQA relationship is too important to be jeopardized by thoughtless lending or borrowing.

Taxes—Render Unto Caesar

As soon as NQA's acquire any income of their own, the government expects to receive its share. Unfortunately, young people do not possess miraculous powers that help them to understand the mysterious ways of the Internal Revenue Service. But then, who does?

But parents often know more than they think, and this is one area where they can state without fear of contradiction that they have had more experience than their children. Parents don't realize how difficult it is for NQA's to get basic information about taxes if it is not provided in the home. Schools rarely teach it. Booklets are on sale in the post office, which attempt to describe everything and are confusing to the uninitiated (and sometimes to the initiated). In the first three months of every year, tax articles appear in the newspapers. Usually they describe changes in the system and are pitched toward those who already are familiar with what they are talking about.

There are books for five-year-olds that describe the reproductive system in great detail, with pictures in living color. But where is the book for 18-year-olds that begins, "This is a W-2 form." However, it is possible to get into almost as much trouble over taxes as sex.

NQA's need to have the importance of the W-2 form explained to them. Often they think tax forms are just something the company does to let the employees know how much money they earned. Early in January, following the first time the NQA is employed, parents should be watching the mail.

Usually the W–2 forms come in tear-off side envelopes and can be recognized. "Sue, this looks like your W–2 form. You'll need it to do your income tax, so put it in a safe place where you'll be able to find it."

NQA's need to be shown how to fill out the tax form and encouraged (but not nagged) to mail them before the deadline. They need instruction, but they learn best by doing it themselves with their parents' guidance.

Parents who have their own taxes computed by a professional can send their NQA's to the same source for information. The young people should go themselves and make their own payments for services received.

If NQA's work where taxes are withheld, having money available to pay taxes when due usually is no problem. Difficulties arise with income from which taxes are not withheld. Many types of employers are not required to withhold. In fact, taxes are not withheld for many of the jobs that are most available to NQA's. Examples are work in small business places, household and farm jobs, waitress or busboy jobs where tips are considered as part of the salary. Workers must make their own reports and payments to the IRS, and the IRS can get quite tense about unreported income.

Parents should encourage NQA's to keep records that can be totaled at the end of the year so that NQA's can see if enough was earned to require a report to the IRS. Some NQA's find it easy to forget their income, but this should not be on the advice of their parents. NQA's should be taught to take every deduction to which they are entitled—but only the legal ones. False reporting to the IRS is a bad habit to establish, for sooner or later it brings disaster.

For most NQA's, income tax work is limited to attaching one or two W–2 statements to the short form, filling in the rest of the blanks, and sending it off. The next step is planning how to spend the refund. If the NQA's do not send the form, the government keeps all the money withheld, and there is no refund.

This is why nagging NQA's to do their income tax is unnecessary. When their friends start cashing their refund checks, it usually comes through to the NQA that he or she is missing something, and the forms are soon in the mail.

Even if nothing gets done, parents should still avoid nagging. "Letting go" in the income tax department means remembering that explanations of what must be done are the parents' responsibility, doing it is the NQA's responsibility, and seeing that it gets done is the government's responsibility. One trip to the IRS office is worth one thousand parental lectures.

Room and Board—Render Unto Parents

In discussions with parents and NQA's, the subject often turns to whether or not NQA's should pay room and board when they live at home. If so, how does one figure out how much? The authors feel that NQA's should make contributions to the household expenses, but that the amount and method of payment will vary according to individual circumstances. NQA's with full-time jobs, for instance, should be charged close to what it would cost them to live outside the home. Parents can check in their community to find out the cost of a room complete with light, heat, and telephone. Add to that the cost of the NQA's food. Require that they pay their own long-distance phone calls and anything else that adds to the cost of running the household as a result of their being there. Do not subtract any amount from what they owe for household chores they may do, if these chores are part of normal maintenance, like mowing the lawn or doing the laundry. This will encourage positive results, such as motivating NQA's to set up their own individual housing arrangements. It also prevents parental resentment from developing against the "kid who takes everything and gives nothing."

Even though the payment is the equivalent of room and board, some parents object to the term because they feel that it gives NQA's the feeling of being a roomer with no responsibility to the household. NQA's who pay for living at home sometimes feel they have a right to complain about services rendered or restrictions placed on their use of the premises. "I'm paying for this room and I'll smoke in it, have whom I want in to visit, and put up any pictures I please!" It is difficult for NQA's to accept the idea that there are also restrictions in rented quarters until they experience this for themselves.

The daughter of the authors discovered this when she wanted to hang some posters in her apartment. She was told that nail holes were not permitted in the newly painted walls. "It's so unfair," she said, "I painted them myself." When the authors' son moved in with some friends, he also came home to discuss his problems. One of the young men sharing the apartment never did the dishes or took out the garbage. . . and so it goes. What a shock it is to discover that parents are sometimes easier to get along with than landlords or even other NQA's!

Years of permissive parenting are difficult to overcome, so some parents feel guilty about taking money from their NQA's. To assuage their guilt, they bank whatever they collect, so that when the young people do move out, a tidy sum is available to buy furniture, pay deposits on rent or telephone, or to pay tuition. At first glance, this looks like a good idea, but it can generate all kinds of trouble, especially if the NQA's are aware of the arrangement. They think it is still their money. They may ask for loans from it or lag behind in their payments. After all, they feel that their parents have asked for money for a specific purpose, but because they are not using it for that purpose, they don't need it. If they are just saving it for their NQA's, use it *now*—for a new car, a trip to Florida over Easter, and so on.

Some parents don't ask for money because they think

that doing so will make it illegal for them to take the young person as a tax deduction as a dependent. Getting around the IRS definition of a dependent in the NQA age range is quite easy because the average NQA's income and student status change frequently. However, the IRS makes it quite clear about who legally can be taken as a dependent. At this writing, if the NQA earns more than $750 per year and is not a full-time student, parents should check carefully to make sure that such a deduction will be allowed. Parents must be able to show that they are providing support that amounts to more than 50% of what the NQA earns. At this time, a full-time job paying the minimum wage held for a full year pays close to $5,000. The NQA who has such a job is probably providing his or her own transportation, spending money, and luxuries. Parents under these circumstances may find it difficult to prove that they provided more than half of the NQA's support.

NQA's should pay *something* for room and board or make *some* contribution to household expenses, or whatever the family wishes to call it. It is no favor to young persons to allow them to keep all their earnings to use as spending money. This permits them to adjust to a standard of living that would be impossible for them to attain on their own resources. NQA's with a good job and a secure future will find that paying room and board helps them to keep a realistic view of the world.

NQA's with low paying jobs need this dose of realism even more. If they are allowed to keep their entire wage to spend on themselves, the money becomes just an enormous allowance. On the other hand, when they must contribute toward their upkeep, they are stimulated to become more economically comfortable, and that means they have to think seriously about their future.

Some NQA's who live at home and work full time do not pay room and board because they are saving for an educational or business goal, which the parents agree is valid and valuable. In this situation, parents should have an understanding that the "free ride" will last for a specific period of time, perhaps six months or a year, depending on how well the NQA lives up to his or her part of the agreement. Parents must be certain that their NQA is using his or her resources to progress toward the agreed-upon goal and is not merely taking advantage of the parents' good nature.

Many young people return home once or twice before they complete their transition from adolescent to adult. When this happens, a financial agreement should be negotiated between them and their parents. There are those who have flunked out of a college they wanted to attend. Some come home because they have been fired or laid off from a job. Some are getting divorced or breaking up what had seemed to be a permanent living arrangement. Others have gotten "goofed up" on drugs (confirmed addicts would be in a different category), or have a temporary health problem. There are many reasons why an NQA may need a moratorium on responsibility, time to lick wounds and regain strength for the next venture into the world. But not too much time!

For whatever the reason, the return home of the NQA is often traumatic for the parents. It is usually unexpected. NQA's seem to announce bad news at awkward times, in the middle of a dinner party or the day before the parents plan to leave on vacation. Many turn up when Mom and Dad are facing a crisis of their own. NQA's find it difficult to believe that anyone over 40 might also lose a job, flunk out of college, have a drug problem, get a divorce, or have trouble with parents—but parents of all ages have problems. NQA's who take this into consideration will be more likely to receive the help they need than those who don't.

With all that may be going on when an NQA returns home, is it possible to be thinking about money too? Certainly! Parents who are in the process of welcoming an NQA should not give the impression that they think he or she is home on anything more than a temporary basis. Contrast the parent who says, "You can stay here as long as you want to stay," with the one who says, "Of course you can stay until you can make better arrangements." Parents should try to give an aura of confidence that they may not necessarily feel. They want to show that, although the NQA may have lost a battle, he or she has not lost the war. Parents can demonstrate this best by their cool assumption that their NQA would not want to become a dependent again, or at least not for a minute longer than is absolutely necessary.

Some time must be allowed for things to cool off. It is important for both the NQA and the parents to take a look at the situation to determine what steps will be necessary so that the NQA can be rerouted toward independence. But, as soon as possible, a detailed discussion must take place regarding the NQA's plans for the future. Somewhere in such a discussion, attempts must be made to reach an agreement on the contribution the NQA will make to the household. Unemployed NQA's might be asked to do more work about the house. Exterior or interior painting jobs are sometimes done for room and board payments. Maybe the basement, attic, or garage could do with a good cleaning.

Adults who live together share the expenses and the maintenance of their living quarters. Parents who wish to have their NQA's act in an adult fashion should show that they expect them to contribute in some way. NQA's who want to be considered fully adult will understand that such a contribution is necessary.

Health Insurance—
Render Unto the Medical Profession

Since NQA's have successfully survived childhood diseases and are not yet prone to the diseases of aging, they may seem incredibly healthy to their parents. And, indeed, they are in the age group least inclined to serious illness. It is so easy to allow time to slide by until one Saturday comes when Mary breaks her leg skiing. Too bad that she turned 20 last Wednesday and is no longer covered by Mom's and Dad's health insurance! Who will pay the doctor and the hospital?

It would be unfair to penalize the NQA's, who undoubtedly assume they are covered if their parents have not told them otherwise. This means that parents who want to avoid this kind of mixup need to do their homework. They must find out exactly when their NQA's go off the family policy.

It would all be a lot easier if all medical insurance policies were the same, but they are not. Some policies will carry a full-time student until age 25. Others have age limits of 18, 19, or 20, or until high school graduation. Some policies cover young persons who work full time and live at home. NQA's who live outside the home but receive partial support are probably not covered, but they might be. Serious problems can arise because the status of the NQA has changed, and no one has considered how the change will affect the health insurance.

The young woman who is getting a divorce had been covered by her husband's policy. Is she now? What about the children? The NQA who was employed full time was under an excellent group health policy, but he got fired. How long does the policy stay in force? Can it be extended? The young person in military service had complete medical care. What is provided after discharge? What about the college student who has decided to take a semester or two off to work or wander? Will the parents' insurance carrier still consider this person a full-time student?

Working NQA's can afford to pay for an occasional visit to the physician and for a prescription. But few people, parents *or* NQA's, find it easy to pay for a week or more in the hospital. In dire circumstances, it may be possible to apply for Title 19 assistance. For specific information, check the local welfare office.

Let's look at a case in point. Twenty-one year old Mary

Ellen was a full-time student. Against her parents' wishes, she moved in with her boy friend. She also dropped several courses and took a part-time job. Three months later she was in the hospital, diagnosed as diabetic. Her two weeks' stay while her insulin dosage was being regulated cost over $3,500.00. When she came to her parents for help, they were as shocked as she was to discover that she was no longer covered by their policy because she was living away from home and was not a full-time student. Her parents were sympathetic, but they told Mary Ellen that they could not pay her medical expenses. They did not feel they should be penalized by the choices she had made.

Mary Ellen became extremely depressed. The disease plus the enormous debt were almost overwhelming. However, she and her boy friend did manage to work it out. Even though she was not employed full time, she was permitted to be included in the group policy where she worked. This helped with the continuing costs of the disease. She applied for and received some help from welfare services. Together, she and her boy friend scrimped and saved to pay off her debt.

Mary Ellen says now that, as difficult as it was, she is glad that her parents treated her as an adult. She is very lucky, however. Her boy friend did not desert her, and her parents maintained a loving relationship even though they were firm in their refusal to commit their income to pay for a problem that Mary Ellen had generated.

Discussions about health insurance policies and how or when they cover a person are an important part of planning for the future. It is not safe to make assumptions. One couple dropped their daughter from their policy when she enrolled in a high-cost college that offered an optional, low-cost group policy to members of its student body. Their thoughtful daughter, thinking she was covered at home, saved them $25.00 a semester by checking "Not Desired" on the insurance application. For three years, no one thought to talk about it, and then she had appendicitis. And so it goes!

Parents should try to teach their NQA's as much as they can about medical coverage. Whatever parents do, NQA's should keep in mind that in the end they are responsible for their own bodies and their own debts.

Educational Costs—You Are Going Where?

Are parents supposed to provide their NQA's with funds to continue their education after high school is completed? How do families decide this issue?

Grandparents, neighbors, the people in the financial aid offices at many colleges, and NQA's sometimes combine in an effort to make parents feel guilty if they do not sacrifice all to send a son or a daughter to the "best school" available.

Difficult though it may be, parents should try to ignore the many pressures that are put upon them. This becomes easier when parents recognize that they alone make the decision as to how much money they will spend to assist a young person to obtain a college education or get advanced job training. That decision is best based on two factors. The first is the parents' ability to pay without undue financial strain. The second is their desire to do so because they feel that they are making a wise investment in the young person's future.

Most parents are more willing to contribute from their income when the NQA's also make a contribution. Some NQA's are not ready to make a commitment in time and effort or in such resources as they can muster. If so, it is wise to wait until they are.

It is also wise to think in terms of *assisting* the young person to go on to school rather than in terms of *sending* him or her. Families that assist rather than send find that education after high school becomes a cooperative venture.

Unfortunately, most planning is not done on the basis of

shared responsibility. It is so much easier to back into a college or training program than it is to confront the multitude of opportunities that are available and to make a realistic choice. We go at it in all the wrong ways.

At very early ages, children are encouraged to talk about potential career choices. "What are you going to be when you grow up?" is a game at six or seven. But in the first years of high school, the game loses its fun and starts to take on a serious aspect. Now, youngsters are told they must make choices—the courses they take NOW, the grades they get NOW, extracurricular activities they participate in NOW, the trouble they get into or stay out of NOW—all this will affect their entire future. But the most important thing is that NOW, they *must figure out what they are going to do* when they grow up, because that mystical moment is not far off.

A few young people are lucky. They know exactly what they want to do, and they have the mental, physical, and financial capabilities to achieve their goals. But most adolescents don't really have a burning desire to do anything specific. Yet, they are constantly reminded, "Soon you are going to graduate. What are you going to do? Choose! NOW!"

A generation or two ago, fewer young people were expected to make such important choices. Many parents made the decisions, and the young people didn't have much to say. The result was occasionally full-scale rebellion, but the current procedure of shifting the major share of the responsibility for career choice to the children has not exactly eliminated revolt. Their job backgrounds are probably limited to frying hamburgers or working on a playground. They probably have not seen Mom or Dad at work, although they may have visited the office. Yet, they are expected to know that they would rather be a nuclear physicist than a naval officer, or a teacher more than they want to be a dairy farmer. Some do, of course, but lots more don't. Young people are handed books listing 10,000 career choices and confronted with library shelves filled with college catalogues. "Choose one," they are told, but what happens when they do make a choice? One day they come home from school all lighted up with joy, and the conversation goes like this:

"Well, I talked to the guidance counselor today, and I've got some really swell news. I've decided I want to be a _____!"

Mom and Dad are really pleased. "That's wonderful," they say. "We're so happy that you made a decision."

"Me, too. It was really tough," answers the young person. "But it's going to be just great. A lot of kids I know are going to the same place."

"Oh, that's nice," the parents say a little doubtfully. "What school are you talking about?"

An expensive college or one in another state is named, and too late the parents realize that they will have problems implementing the decision that the young person has been urged to make. They begin to ask if it is possible to study the same subject in a college closer to home. Maybe a state-supported institution would be more practical than a private school. Are there jobs available in the field after graduation? Perhaps the NQA could seek a more realistic career choice at a cheaper place.

Now the son or daughter begins to react angrily in an attempt to present a defense. "Boy, you're really ripping me off. You tell me to figure it out, and when I do, it turns out to be all wrong. . . . Why didn't you tell me what you wanted me to do in the first place?"

It is a legitimate question, even though we have a great deal of sympathy for parents who fall into this trap.

There are many questions to be answered before a family chooses a college or job training school.

How much of the parents' income are they willing and able to commit to the project? Perhaps they cannot afford any cash contribution at all. Maybe they can promise free room and board to an NQA who is attending a local school. What outside means of support are available?

How much will the student contribute? Can he or she
work part time? In the summer? Is he or she eligible for
grants, scholarships, or low-interest loans? Does the young
person have any savings to contribute? Will he or she sell
something (usually a car) and put the proceeds toward the
first year's tuition?

What are the relative costs at publicly supported institutions as compared with private schools?

How much will transportation cost?

What will personal expenses amount to?

Would it be wise to work for a year and save some money
before going on to school?

What kind of GI Bill does the military offer these days?
Is this a possible way to obtain support?

The various colleges and schools should be visited. The
financial aid office at each should be visited at the same time.

After parents have made it clear how much support they
are able to provide, NQA's can be left to make decisions. If
they still want to go to the expensive private school in another
state and they can figure out a way to pay for it, why not let
them go? It is, however, a good idea also to check the situation at Hometown U. in case the scholarship or the summer
job falls through.

A word here about loans for continuing education. They
come in two varieties. There are the kinds made by the local
bank, which carry high interest rates and require payment in
a short time. They have the advantage of being available, but
they are costly. There are also government loans, which bear
low interest. Repayment on these usually starts after the
student is out of school and can be made over periods of 10 or
more years. This kind of loan used to be available only to
low-income families, but the government guidelines vary
from year to year. Many middle-income families now qualify.

Some people think it is only thoughtless, uncaring parents who allow their NQA's to borrow money for education.
"You are making them mortgage their whole future," they

say. But, if anybody has to mortgage their future, why not the NQA's? Their future extends over a much longer time period.

When a decision is reached and the division of responsibility for costs is established, this should be considered a one-year contract between the parents and the NQA, with an option to renew if the student's performance in school merits renewal, if the grants or loans are still available, and if the parents' financial circumstances have remained the same. The amount of assistance from the family may increase or decrease depending on resources gained or reversals suffered. NQA's constantly should be seeking new financial resources for themselves.

Whatever the parents decide to contribute should be deposited in the NQA's checking account. An NQA can then make the payments from the account to the school. For a beginning student, deposits to the bank account are best made on a quarterly basis. Some prefer monthly. This will allow NQA's less opportunity to blow next semester's tuition on a present fancy. Seniors and graduate students are probably adept enough at financial management to handle the money all in one chunk if this is an advantage to the parents, but freshmen and sophomores are not usually that experienced.

Many pitfalls wait to trap unwary families. Education after high school always costs more than one thinks it is going to, because *something* always happens. The budding engineer's calculator is stolen. Bedding and towels go to the laundry and never return. Laboratory fees are higher this year than the catalog stated. The guaranteed campus job pays 40¢ less per hour than was thought. The landlord is raising the rent or the roommate has disappeared, taking the silverware and dishes, but leaving behind a $50.00 long-distance phone bill. A $300.00 microscope has been dropped. By the time NQA's are seniors, they can be expected to plan for and take care of their own emergencies, but only if parents begin to show them how when they are freshmen. Parents should set aside something for emergencies and should help out only with the really unexpected variety, not the ones that are the result of inexperience and foolishness, or actions taken by NQA's in opposition to parents' wishes or advice.

Disasters that are the result of youth and inexperience do occur. Take George, for example. He did well during his freshman year at the state university. He worked at two jobs during the summer and cleared more than $1,200.00 Terrific! But his parents were totally unprepared to find out that George had gone to the racetrack with some friends, had a bit to drink, and lost all the money that he had saved for next year's college costs—more than $900.00 down the drain. Now he is sitting in the living room in tears, vowing he will never again do such a stupid thing. He says he has learned a lesson, and very likely he has. But he is still $900.000 short. Who gets to pay the cost of George's valuable lesson?

Parents may feel hardhearted when they tell George to take a semester off and work to make up the money he wasted so foolishly. But if they do not do this, they will be paying George's gambling debts for him. They also will not have given George the opportunity, difficult as it is, to learn what it means to suffer the consequences of one's own actions.

George may not react with joy either. The tears of remorse can change rapidly to hard-eyed threats, slammed doors, and other expressions of hostility. It is not easy on the parents, nor is it easy on the NQA who has demonstrated so vividly that he is not yet as adult as he thought. No one likes to make a fool out of oneself, no matter the age.

Another pitfall for unwary parents is illustrated by the following case: Susan worked as a waitress in a summer resort. She has returned home with $950.00 and the usual bag of dirty laundry. After doing the wash and eating supper, Susan is sitting with her parents discussing the coming year.

"I guess I told you that Mary Beth and Helen are going to take the second semester off and go to Europe," Susan says. "And I've decided that I want to go too. I'll never get another chance like this. Helen's aunt lives in Paris, and we can stay with her. All I'll have to pay is my way over and for some food. They tell me I can get a job as a waitress or something too, so I can pick up some spare change. I'll just take the money for this summer to pay my way, and it won't cost you a cent because you'll pay just the same amount as you would if I were going to go for the full year. I mean, you pay the usual amount you pay for the whole year for the first semester, because I'll be saving mine for the trip and then I take the second semseter off, and it won't cost you a thing—see what I mean?"

"All too well," Susan's father replies. "You are going to spend $950.00 to go to Europe, and we get to pay twice as much as we said we would for one semester of school."

"No, Dad," Susan explains. "I'm not going to go the second semester, so it comes out that you spend exactly the same amount."

"You mean that you're going to work it out with the university to get through in three and a half years? That's not likely, Susan! Sooner or later you'll want to complete that second semester, and sooner or later you're going to want our help for it."

Mother continues. "So, darling, if you want to go to Europe, that's fine with us. But we'll still pay just what we planned to pay for the first semester and save the rest for when you get back. I do hope you can work it out. It sounds like a wonderful opportunity."

Susan is probably in tears at this point. "You never let me do anything even with my own money!" she says. But the chances are she will be able to work out the arrangements for the trip if she really wants to go. NQA's who want to do something are very resourceful. Families who recognize this are well on their way toward managing the financial problems that arise as adolescents progress into adulthood.

Along with obtaining and holding a permanent job, the

most important mark of adulthood is the ability to manage one's own finances. On the other hand, it is difficult for parents, especially permissive ones, to see their NQA's as adults when it comes to finances. NQA's do not make this easier. They find it very comfortable to remain financially dependent on their parents. But letting go and getting free mean that parents outgrow their feelings of financial obligation, their need to sacrifice, their desire to be needed. Letting go and getting free mean that NQA's outgrow their need to be dependent, give up their expectations to receive everything and give little in return, to be cared for at all times.

Adult relationships are based on choice and cooperation, on reciprocal relationships. When members of families let go of immature expectations, they become free to build these reciprocal relationships in which each member gives as much as he or she receives.

REFERENCES

[1]J.J. Conger, *Adolescence and Youth* (New York; Harper and Row, 1973), pp. 161–62.

Conflicts
in
Life-Styles

Differences over what is appropriate personal conduct is a common characteristic of parent–NQA relationships. These differences involve the nature of membership in the family group. Sociologists describe two major forms of enduring group relationships. The type of group that exists primarily to provide personal support for its members is called a *primary group*. The group that exists because its members have a common task to perform is called a *secondary group*. The family of origin and family of marriage are important examples of primary groups. Other examples are fraternity and sorority groups, buddy groups, gangs, or certain types of religious groups. In these groups, individual members are very important to each other, and each has an important effect on the behavior of the other.

The persons one works with at the office, the factory, or in the classroom are examples of secondary groups. There may be some personal relationships that develop, but these will be related to the work that has to be performed. Most of the relationships with members of secondary groups are limited to those that take place in the setting where the activity is performed. We will not discuss secondary group relationships in this book, because we are discussing the family. It is necessary to keep the distinction in mind, however, for every person carries out the majority of his or her personal relationships in these two types of groups. Each group places certain demands on its members and extends certain rights because of membership in the group.

When children are young, their family of origin is the most important group in their lives. They look for approval from their parents for most of what they do. Parents express their opinions of their children's behavior and then expect their children to conduct themselves according to the parents' wishes. When children grow older, they become members of primary groups in addition to the family. This membership of children in other groups claims allegiance from them. If the expectations of the members of their other groups place them in conflict with their family group, children will find themselves having to make choices, which in turn causes further conflict with one or the other of the groups. Most of the time when this happens to younger children, they either drop out of the competing groups or give priority to the expectations of the family. Conflict is thereby minimized.

One of the major tasks for NQA's is to let go and get free from excessive demands of the family of origin. This means forming close personal relationships in other primary groups and establishing new primary groups in which the NQA has a prominent place. Often, as a result of these group affiliations, NQA's will behave in ways that distress parents. NQA's think of themselves as adults. They resent parents' harping on the way they dress, what they eat, how they talk, the music they listen to, the way they view religion. When parents observe these changes, their first reaction is to try to bind the NQA's close into the family group and to question their friends. In most parents' minds, their NQA's behavior is directly related to their friends.

The conflicts in life-styles that we will discuss later in this chapter arise from parents seeing NQA's as belonging *primarily* to the family and subject *primarily* to the family's behavioral expectations; whereas NQA's feel they are adult enough to make their own decisions about what company they keep and the way they conduct themselves. When this kind of conflict becomes intense, parents will go to extreme lengths to keep their NQA's under their domination. NQA's will go to equal lengths to escape.

Some parents worry when the NQA becomes involved in certain types of religions. Others worry about drugs. The counterculture lurks in some parents' minds as a threat. A change in political affiliation can upset a family. Fears that panic some seem trivial to others. A leader in the women's liberation movement can be as upset when her daughter wants to settle down and raise a family as a traditional housewife might be if her daughter decided to try for West Point. One family's threat can be another family's goal. With the amount of diversity in style, values, and taste that exists in groups in the United States, it is not surprising that differences of opinion about how life should be lived should arise in families too.

Cohabitation, drugs, and religious sects provide relationships that worry parents, but they do not generally worry the young people who are involved with them. Some NQA's are aware that there are risks in some of the things they are doing, and they are prepared to accept the consequences. Other NQA's have heard so much about risks from their parents and other adults that they reject the very existence of any threat.

Parents, with their experience and their concern for their children, often see too many dangers. NQA's with their idealism and their attitude that "it may happen to others, but it won't happen to me," tend to overlook most dangers. The interaction of these one-sided viewpoints is rather like the conditions that cause an earthquake, where two plates of the earth move in opposite directions with all kinds of upheaval on the fault line (or the "no fault" line, depending which side the contending parties are on).

The situation today, if different at all from times past, is different only in form, not in function. Children must still move away from their family of origin toward groups in which they can work toward maturity. This process can cause distress to the members of the family. We will discuss four kinds of behavior that reflect the standards of the groups with which young persons affiliate and around which conflicts of style can arise. They are: cohabitation with a member of the opposite sex; homosexual relationships; membership in religious cults; and use of drugs.

Cohabitation

During the NQA period, young people generally begin to form the special kind of relationship with a member of the opposite sex that will lead to establishment of the family of marriage, the new home, the new family group. What was only one's son or daughter is getting ready also to become a husband or wife and a father or mother, a group separate from the family of origin. For many parents, this is a culmination of their child-rearing efforts. They look forward to spoiling the grandchildren and hope to feel that they have not lost a child but gained one. They hope that their child will be the one who dates sufficiently to acquire knowledge about the types of choices of available partners; who, at a suitable age, has a period of serious courtship followed by an engagement that gives a sufficient amount of time to get the wedding invitations printed; and that the grandchildren will not begin to arrive in less than one year. Of course, divorce is never anticipated.

This hope of most parents—that their child will not break off relationship with the primary family group, but that the group will expand to include new members and all will continue to be one happy family—is not too often fulfilled. Marriage is not the only way in which an individual can relate to another person. Families in all periods of history have had to accept the fact that their children had developed loyalties that the parents could accept or reject, but to which the children were themselves committed.

"This is Vicky's . . . uh . . . er . . . boy . . . well, er . . . boy friend." "Jim is coming home and bringing his . . . well . . . uh . . . well, I guess you could say his fiancée."

You could say that, but the folks who are listening probably are aware that the tentative introduction means that if Jim and his "fiance," or Vicky and her "boyfriend" set a wedding date, shower gifts won't really be necessary. The happy couple has been furnishing the apartment for some time now.

Even though parents may think so, cohabitation is not something their sons and daughters have thought up in the last 10 or so years just to plague them. It has been around since Adam and Eve. A whole body of law grew up around common law marriage, but that form of marriage is outlawed in most states. The trial marriage was thought up in the 1920s, but it didn't get too far in the way of popular acceptance. Then, as now, people who lived together just sort of lived together. They did not want the relationship referred to by a name that did not express their personal reasons for sharing housing.

In the past few years, living together has become far more common than it was in the earlier part of the twentieth century. Between 1970–76, the number of men and women living together without a wedding license more than doubled. As of March 1976, the Census Bureau reported that more than 1,300,000 unmarried Americans lived with a member of the opposite sex.[1] The number is probably larger than the statistics show. The Bureau's figures include only those couples who have been together long enough to become part of their statistics. It is impossible for them to include those living arrangements that bloom and wither away in less than a year.

Cohabitation is not a cooperative house or a commune. Nor is it a brief encounter. A man and a woman who live together under the same roof, have a sexual relationship, and are not legally married are cohabiting. Some couples have plans to get married at a future date. Some would say "maybe." Others have absolutely no intention of getting married—ever. Not all are NQA's, although this life-style is far more common for those under 35 than for those over 35. However, living together is not unheard of in any age group, including senior citizens.

People who choose to cohabit instead of getting legally married often say that their decision to do so is based on their personal value system. To many, the most important thing is their personal commitment to each other, and this, they say, would not be improved by a piece of paper or a bit of religious ritual. Some do not wish to get married because they feel that in this way they will avoid the personal and legal trauma of a divorce if they decide to break up. For many, cohabitation is a matter of convenience. They do not wish to make a long-term commitment that would prevent them from migrating to another locality or another partner when they feel like it. Others are testing their relationship to see if they do wish to get married. Some don't get married because they pay less taxes that way. Whatever the reason expressed, people who live together without marriage usually can give reasons why they feel that doing so is the right thing for them at a particular time.

The majority of people over 35, a group that includes most all parents of NQA's, feel that living together is not right, no matter what reasons are given. When asked what they think about it, parents tend to knit their brows and look worried. Some consider cohabitation to be highly immoral. They call it "living in sin." To others, it is dangerous. "Isn't it illegal?" they ask. Some believe it is frivolous or irresponsible. "After all, what if she gets pregnant?" or "They are just fooling around, not making a commitment," they say.

Many parents are embarrassed by the living arrangements of their children. They worry that others in the community will think they have failed to do a good job of instilling their children with proper moral values. "After all," they say, "what will people think?"

These parents believe that the only way they can effectively demonstrate to the community that they disapprove of the relationship is to break off all contact with the cohabiting NQA. When there are other children in the family, a clincher is added to the argument. "If I don't break off the relationship with my child who is living in sin, it will seem to the other children that I approve, and they will think it is all right with me if they do the same thing. I must make my position clear to everyone."

Jim has been living with Claudia for two years. His mother died 10 years ago, and his father brought up Jim and two younger sisters. Ever since Jim and Claudia moved in together, his father has cut off all contact with him. Furthermore, he has ordered the two younger sisters to stay away from Jim. The father says that he must protect the younger children by making it clear exactly how he feels about Jim's living arrangement.

But the youngest daughter, age 18, says this is "the silliest thing I have ever seen. I know how my Dad feels, and I respect his opinion. But," she continues, "I know how I feel too, and I'm not going to give up my relationship with my brother no matter what he says.

"So, you know how we work it out? I just tell Dad that I'm going to work late at the library or visit a friend, and then I go see Jim and Claudia. What makes me mad is that Dad has put me in a position where I have to lie to him. That's not very moral. And he knows I go to visit Jim because sometimes he asks me about them. That's real hypocrisy, and I think that's worse than lying or even living with a guy.

"Doesn't Dad know I have a mind of my own? If they had gotten married instead, I wouldn't have rushed out and grabbed a husband anymore than I'm going to look for some guy to shack up with just because Jim is living with Claudia.

"Anyway, I think Dad is just using that talk about protecting us younger kids to hide some problem of his own. Maybe he is just mad because he can't make Jim do what he says anymore."

Maybe the father does have a hidden motive in this case. It is more likely that he is acting in what he thinks are truly the best interests of his family, but he has not considered the side effects of his action. There are ways other than breaking off the relationship that might have proved more effective in stating his case against cohabitation.

Jim's father could have achieved his purpose by telling Jim and Claudia and the younger sisters that he disapproved of living together without marriage. He should give his reasons for his disapproval clearly and concisely. At the same time, he should make it clear that he knows it is Jim's decision and, therefore, whatever happens as a result is also Jim's responsibility. The father can say that he loves Jim even while he disapproves of what he is doing. It will not be necessary for the father to repeat his objections constantly to either the younger children or to Jim. They'll know.

Nor does the father have to permit them to sleep together in his house or to provide financial support to maintain their living arrangement.

Finally, if a nosy neighbor says, "Say, what's going on with Jim and Claudia? You must be worried sick about them," the father can answer, "Jim is of age, and he makes his own decisions. What he does is not my business . . . so it certainly is none of yours!"

This is not to suggest that Jim's father should have a change of heart and start saying things like, "Wow, that's wonderful, what you're doing. You kids get all the breaks." Far from it. But sometimes NQA's are not content with a simple acknowledgment that they are old enough to make their own decisions. They want more. They want assurances from their parents that, regardless of what they are doing, they are still wonderful, wonderful, even as when they were younger they wanted Mom and Dad to cheer for them at games, clap for them in plays, and tell them what super kids they are. Long after parents have given up trying to get NQA's to behave in a certain way, the NQA's are trying to get their parents to behave in ways that the NQA's think are right. NQA's want to be adults who make their own decisions, but often they do not want to allow their parents the same freedom.

"I don't see why my Mom and Dad won't let me sleep with Jane when we visit them," Matthew said. "They know what our relationship is. Boy, are they ever hypocrites not to be open about it like we are."

Hold on. Who is the hypocrite?

Undoubtedly, the parents do know about the relationship, and, equally undoubtedly, they do not think that living together outside of marriage is right. They have accepted the fact that they cannot force their opinion on their son, but he is still trying to force his opinion on them. He wants not only to live with his friend, but also to have his parents come over to his way of thinking.

Furthermore, the son wants to use the parents' home as though it belonged to him. This issue of whether to permit the sharing of the bed in the old homestead also relates back to the earlier discussion on territory. After the NQA moves out of the parents' home and into a home of his or her own, the parents' home becomes their exclusive territory, even as the NQA's new residence is unavailable territory to the parents. Hopefully, both parents and NQA's always will be welcome visitors in each others' homes, but each has to accept the others' autonomy in their own territory. If parents are made uncomfortable by the idea of having an unmarried couple sharing a bed in their home, the young people should be neither surprised nor hurt. If the NQA's cannot bear to be separated for a night or two, they can get a room in a motel.

Parents who spend some time visiting a cohabiting child can expect to see the couple retiring to the bedroom. If this unsettles the parents, they can take a room in a motel, but they should not expect the cohabiters to sleep apart during their visit.

Both parents and NQA's are entitled to keep and act upon their own value systems. Parents let go when they accept the idea that children can still love them even if they do not always conform to their wishes. NQA's must let go too. Their parents do still love them even when they do not always agree with NQA's "own" decisions.

When families discuss cohabitation only in terms of morality, the other problems that cohabitation can present are not considered. The parents' task of helping the NQA to obtain information that will help to minimize risks is left incomplete.

Cohabiters often say that they do so because if they break up they will avoid all the legal and emotional hassles of a divorce. This statement is idealistic, but it is not realistic. A problem-free split is definitely not guaranteed by cohabitation.

It takes two to make a relationship. It only takes one to break it up. If one person wants to split and the other does not, it doesn't matter whether or not they are legally married—the breakup can be emotionally devastating. The one who wants to make the break often feels guilty for the pain he or she is causing a formerly loved partner. Both parties often experience a sense of personal failure. The one who does not want to break up feels unloved; the other feels incapable of forming a good relationship with another individual. "What's the matter with me? Everytime I fall in love, the guy (or girl) turns out to be a domineering stinker. There must be something I'm doing wrong."

There is also the loneliness. It doesn't matter much to a single who used to double whether the partner was removed by death, divorce, or just packed up and moved out one day. The grief is very similar in all three circumstances. Even when the two have agreed to separate, they each must become accustomed to a new way of life. Friends must be told. Ways of relating to others must be worked out.

The emotional aspects of separation do not depend on the legality of marriage. In fact, since the expectations a couple has for a cohabiting relationship are often higher than those assigned to a marriage, the emotional trauma of a break is sometimes even more severe.

Does cohabitation assure that all legal problems will be avoided? Certainly not, particularly if the couple has any property to divide or has produced a child.

The legal problems of a divorce are at least standardized by each state, and when the relationship is broken, the individuals involved have some idea of what their rights and obligations are going to be. On the other hand, in the breakup of a living-together arrangement, people are often surprised to find that, although they are outside the protection of many of the laws, they are not outside the *need* for protection.

Consider, for instance, the couple who shared an apartment and planned to get married the following year. They announced their engagement and began to purchase home furnishings. They also opened a joint savings account. In it they deposited nearly $4,000.00. But the relationship did not grow. One day one of the partners came home to find the apartment bare. The savings account was also bare, and there turned out to be no way to recover either a share of the money or the furniture.

If children are born to a cohabiting couple, the potential for problems at the time of a breakup is even greater, since the positions of both parents and children before the law are poorly defined. Recent court decisions have given more rights to both unwed fathers and mothers, but this has served to confuse the issues rather than straighten them out.

Legal marriages are defined by laws written and passed by the legislatures of the 50 states. On the other hand, legal precedents governing cohabitation are in the process of being developed by the courts.

People who are living together do not share in many benefits that come to the officially married. For instance, they usually cannot live in a university's married student's housing. Cohabiters are not eligible for their partners' health insurance, pension plans, and social security benefits. Since many companies are inclined to have somewhat conservative, middle-aged leadership, cohabiting may affect one's chances of promotion. Cohabiters think discriminations of this sort are unfair and are taking their protests to court. This has the effect of bringing cohabitation out of its obscure, ill-defined position and into the open. This also has the tendency to destroy its original concept of free and easy living. The more court cases there are that settle property and children's rights, and the more that cohabiters insist on being recognized as a legitimate relationship by society, the more a body of law and precedent will build up around this type of relationship. At the same time, many of the legal difficulties of divorce are being lessened by passage of "no fault" divorce laws.

As divorce laws are liberalized and cohabitation laws become formalized, a gradual convergence between the two is taking place. The same protections and, therefore, the same limitations to freedom may soon be provided to both relationships. In the future, the legal problems of breaking up will be predictable. At present, the fact that they are unpredictable does not mean that they do not exist. Couples that make the assumption that they are avoiding all legal problems by living together without getting married can be in for some very unpleasant surprises.

Homosexual Relationships

Some parents would be overjoyed to find out that their son or daughter is living with a member of the opposite sex. These parents are not necessarily expressing nontraditional values. It is only that they have discovered that there is something they disapprove of even more than cohabitation. Their NQA has just announced that he or she is more at ease in a homosexual relationship. To many parents, this is the most repugnant situation imaginable.

As with cohabitation, parents feel shame and embarrassment. What can they tell their friends or relatives? If they accept the NQA's behavior, will it not seem that they approve this kind of relationship? Anyway, doesn't the Bible define homosexuality as a sin? What effect will this have on the other children in the family?

Added to these reactions is one of intense disappointment. This young person will not be getting married, and so the parents' aspirations that the family will be extended must be scrapped. Homosexual children do not produce grandchildren, nor are they likely to purchase a lovely suburban home, pictures of which the parents can show with pride to friends and neighbors. Furthermore, if the person's sexual preference is revealed, opportunities in many job categories will be limited. This is quite a lot for parents to handle.

Added to all this is the guilt that many parents experience. Traditional explanations place all the blame on the parents. Mother was too domineering or too cold or too close to her child or too something else. Father was too passive or too aggressive or too rejecting or put too much emphasis on success. In some way, whatever they did or however they did it, parents are made to feel that it was their child rearing methods that have produced the "gay" in the family. Many parents feel that they have caused an abnormality to occur, and so they think they must bring about a cure. Since many homosexuals do not consider themselves sick, and therefore do not desire a cure, parental attempts in this direction heighten the conflict.

"Gayness" is a style of life, related to membership in a primary group that supports such behavior. The reasons why some choose to be "gay" and others do not are not agreed upon by either the medical profession or the social scientists. The type of parenting a person has had may be one of the contributing factors. It is only one of many.

Sometimes, when NQA's say they are homosexual, they are not making a positive statement based on a long-term commitment to a way of life. Instead, it may be that they are asking a question—they have had a homosexual experience or two, which they found pleasurable, and they want their parents to help them straighten out what it all means. Parents can explain that an individual is never required to wear a label for the rest of his or her life. If parents insist on attaching the label homosexual to their NQA, they also tend to confirm the behavior and make it nearly impossible for the individual to change his or her mind. Many young people have participated in homosexual relationships, and in later life they found that they preferred a straight relationship with a member of the opposite sex.[2] And of course, a certain number remain gay throughout their lives. Many do not hide their sexual preferences and are active in "gay lib." This is often heartbreaking for parents who feel that if they maintain close ties with their homosexual son or daughter, it will appear to other members of the family, to the community, and maybe even to themselves, that they approve of homosexuality.

Upsets in families occur because family members feel that since they all share a certain amount of the same genes and experiences, all family members should be just alike. But it doesn't work out that way. It is possible for a convict to have a priest for a brother, genius can share space at the dinner table with the retarded, and a gay son or daughter can turn up at the weddings of the other (heterosexual) children in the family. At birth, children begin the process of forming separate identities. This process is completed during the NQA years. The establishment of separate identities also establishes separate responsibility for one's acts. Parents no longer need to feel they are accountable for everything NQA's do, every mistake they make, every relationship they form.

The same kinds of thoughts that applied to cohabiting couples apply here, too.

Homosexuality is an emotional subject and lengthy discussions about its acceptability, whether initiated by parents or NQA's, are more likely to lead to further arguments than to settlements of the differences of opinion. The most important thing is that parents and NQA's both appreciate that, even though these differences of opinion exist, the family relationship can continue.

Cults

From time to time in history, new religions or variations of old religions have challenged those already established. These new religions caused great conflict until they were either discarded by their adherents or accepted by the majority. Christianity is an example. It challenged the older Jewish and pagan orders. For several centuries, Christian believers suffered a variety of persecutions at the hands of nonbelievers.

A major development in Christianity caused almost as much conflict. The Reformation was violently contested, and many on both sides were burned at the stake or racked to death before Protestants and Catholics learned to coexist. Today, in Ireland, remnants of that struggle are still in evidence.

There are religions that did not make it, or lasted only

briefly until the adherents were killed, died off, or were reabsorbed into the mainstream. Examples include the Shakers and the Perfectionists.

Mormonism flourishes today, but its beginnings were marked with lynchings, burnings, and other persecutions as Joseph Smith and his followers moved west in search of a place where the religious freedom promised by the Constitution could be practiced.

Throughout history, diversity in thought has existed about what kind of life occurs after this one is finished. If the discussions were merely about the next life, they would not have provoked much conflict, for one's present actions would not be involved. However, discussions are centered not so much on what may happen, but on the best way to assure the desired result. Conflicts occur when there is disagreement about how a person must behave in this world to achieve life in the next.

At the present time in America, many new religious ideas are being offered, all of which demand a certain type of conduct on the part of believers. They range from a Messianic form of Christianity complete with a new Messiah to the assorted exportations of Eastern thought. Some of these are no doubt based on sincere religious commitment. Others are less idealistic in orientation and more dedicated to life in this world and the profit motive. In the midst of a religious revival, it is difficult, if not impossible, to tell which is which.

There is very little literature on sects such as the Unification Church that is not produced by people who are either violently in favor of it or violently opposed to Reverend Moon. The Hare Krishna, the Children of God, The Way, The Walk, Scientology, and others have attracted similar outpourings of support and damnation.

The only thing that seems certain about these sects is that, although their membership includes people of all ages, their efforts at evangelization are directed to the 18–25 age group. It is difficult to tell how successful they have been.

Membership in each of the individual groups rarely exceeds 10,000, but this membership is only estimated, and there are many groups. Some writers estimate the total membership in all these cults to be close to one million persons.[3]

Of the newer sects, the various Christian cults and the Hare Krishna are most feared by parents because of the evangelizing methods used. The charge has been made that believers are not really believers at all. Rather, they are said to be victims of brainwashing and mind control, which turn them into robots doing the will of a leader who controls them in various fund-raising efforts and uses the profits gained by their toil to live in luxury. It is said that one can detect their robotness in the fact that they smile constantly and react abnormally when insulted; that they do not become angry or violent, but only smile all the harder.

It would be very useful, if it could be said without misgivings, that the above charges are either true or false. Possibly the reason this cannot be done is that the charges are both true and false. Some of the members of the cults are undoubtedly true believers. Others are kept in line by group pressure. Whether the kind of pressure exerted by the group constitutes mind control or brainwashing is not agreed upon by the specialists.

Why parents react so fearfully to the type of group pressure applied in certain cults, but do not get enraged when many of the same tactics are used by branches of the military, is interesting to consider. Perhaps this is because no matter how difficult it is to get out during one's period of enlistment, time does eventually pass, and the soldier, sailor, or marine is given the choice of whether or not to re-enlist. At present, many believe that the opportunity to deny or reaffirm commitment is not assured by the various cults.

The deprogramming process is supposed to provide the individual with this opportunity. By this method, parents hire people to abduct the cult member and subject him or her to intensive pressure to give up the newly acquired faith.

When the various cults began, some of them recruited members who were under the age of legal majority. When the courts backed up the parents and permitted them to take their children back home, the cults stopped active recruiting among the underaged and began to concentrate on NQA's. This did not prevent indignant parents from attempting to reclaim their children, but it has hampered their efforts since the courts have found it necessary to question where religious freedom stops and mind control begins. The courts are asked to decide whether mind control (deprogramming) as exercised by parents is more or less restricting to individuals than the mind control (group pressure) exercised by a cult. Lawyers for both parents and cults argue that they represent the side that permits real freedom of choice.

In some cases deprogramming has worked well. The former cult member heaved a great sigh of relief and returned to the family. In other cases, the person who was being deprogrammed pretended to have given up his or her beliefs only until the parents' backs were turned, and then he or she skipped off to rejoin the cult. The majority of deprogrammings result in a condition called "floating." The deprogrammed person does not rejoin the cult, but seems unable to find anything else of interest. They are caught in the conflict over life-styles that can result from simultaneous membership in conflicting groups.

Drug Use

NQA's have grown up with drug use even as they have grown up with television, affluence, inflation, and the American ethic of child-centeredness. Most have experience with mind-altering substances. The extent of this experience is beyond the comprehension of most parents. This is not to say that all NQA's use drugs, although the majority have done some experimentation, but they are familiar with the effects of drugs. They know people who are casual users, some who are more than casual users, and some who have developed drug dependence. During adolescence, they assist friends who were coming off bad trips, and they are familiar with schoolyard pushers who market the stuff. They know the difference between a real pusher and the next-door neighbor kid who has made a run to some location where drugs are sold in quantity and brought back a little extra for friends. All this and more they have learned before they reached 17 and became an NQA.

This doesn't mean that anyone who is ever going to be an addict is already one by 18, or that parents can stop being concerned about drug use. It does mean that parents have less to worry about than many realize. Most NQA's are not innocent babes in the drug woods, who are likely to be taken in by new forms of temptation if they move to their own apartment or go away to school.

Parents express two concerns about drugs, both of which revolve around the risks taken by the user. The first is what is a particular drug likely to do to the user? Will the user become addicted? The second worry is what will happen if the person who is using a controlled substance for the fun of it gets caught by the police? Will the NQA be fined or put in jail? Will his or her future be ruined by a police record or addiction?

On the other hand, most drug users feel that mind-altering substances produce a lot of good feelings and don't do any real harm. They are sure that they know the risks involved. They are aware of the dangers of addiction to some drugs and consider others to be habituating but not addicting. They are also familiar with the local representatives of the Drug Enforcement Administration and have a pretty good idea about what the local police force will put up with and what they are likely to bet busted for. They feel that they have examined the risks and that these are more than balanced by the benefits.

NQA's who use drugs do so because they choose to do so. Peer pressure does not force them into regular use, but use does force the individual into membership in groups that share the activity. Since use of many drugs is an illegal act, those who do so protect each other's use in order that all may avoid problems with the police. NQA's who illegally use drugs rationalize their behavior by adopting a system of belief about the brotherhood of those who use drugs. In other words, they become committed to membership in a group.

The authors do not make the same assumption about human behavior that most of the family watchers do. Family watchers start from the position that abnormality is the most common attribute of social existence. They assume that individuals and society are oriented toward problems; that life is a struggle against internal and external forces that may at any time overwhelm the individual; that a certain psychological and social bleakness is the lot of mankind. The position of these family watchers is very close to the theological doctrine of original sin.

The authors proceed from the assumption that most persons do an adequate job of managing themselves during their lives. Most persons are reasonably content with their circumstances. Most persons live an orderly existence and are fairly satisfied with the conditions of society about them. When difficulties arise in the lives of most people, they may suffer some, but eventually they will make the accommodation necessary to keep their lives going in reasonable balance.

People should be careful to evaluate the problems that are presented by the family watchers through the media so that they do not conclude that problems are the average condition. Normal situations do not make good news—problem situations do. But problems, whether natural catastrophes, personal tragedies, or individuals gone mad, are the exception, not the rule. Most people, regardless of age, live life quietly, by the rules, trying to do their best as they perceive the best to be.

It would have been much easier to describe the conflicts of life-style in terms of personality problems on the part of NQA's than in terms of group affiliation. But to use the common analysis that the individual is the sole factor in any social behavior is at best oversimplification and at worst mischievous. Placing the total responsibility at the feet of the person involved in problem behavior also gives the people involved in the behavior a false sense that the problem can be solved by administering some sort of psychological elixir to the individual, and control will be reasserted. Solution to conflicts is only partially possible by concentration on the internal aspects of an individual's personality. As we have said often, the major portion of difficulties that arise are difficulties of social relationships. Any satisfactory solution to these difficulties must be developed by concentrating on the social relationships involved, not by concentrating on the personalities involved.

When conflicts in life-styles arise, it is necessary for parents and NQA's to keep in mind that they are normal, adequately functioning individuals. The conflicts arise from differences in tastes, rules, and habits, which result from the groups one affiliates with. In the case of parents, they have lived with the same persons for so long that what they have been doing as a result of being with these persons becomes their own ways of behaving. And since NQA's have been living with parents for a number of years and have been doing what parents want them to do, parents think that NQA behavior comes from inside the NQA instead of from the controls that parents have been exerting. When NQA's change their lifestyle, parents take this change as a slap at themselves and become hurt, angry, and often punitive. They may even think that their NQA's have gone through a basic personality change that may make them different from the rest of the family forever. And then the parents may lose their ability to think things through clearly, and they may resort to hostile, coercive behavior. Oftentimes when this happens, parents alienate themselves from their NQA's, and thereby reduce the possibility of overcoming the conflicts of life-style. Of, if parents can overpower their NQA's by forcing them to withdraw from the behavior in contention, parents are also forcing their NQA's to withdraw from friends that are important to them. The result can be personal alienation, which we will discuss in the next chapter, or development of other kinds of conflicts between parents and their children.

Parents must be careful that in their fear for their NQA's they do not, by their actions, drive the NQA's more tightly into membership in the groups that parents want them to leave. One of the ways to minimize this tendency is to view the conflicting life-style as temporary, as part of growing up. This is very easy to say and very difficult to do. But time heals many things. By the time people reach 30, their behavior more nearly than not resembles that of their parents. In other words, behavior tends to be conservative. That which is first learned tends to reassert itself.

It is very difficult for parents and NQA's alike to avoid the "throwing the baby out with the bath" syndrome. Parents tend to equate their dislike of NQA's behavior with dislike of NQA's themselves. NQA's tend to turn their backs on parents when they object to how their parents treat them if they behave in ways their parents dislike. During the NQA period, it is very important to separate "not liking the behavior" from "not liking the person exhibiting that behavior." Neither parents nor NQA's have to approve of each other's behavior, but if they do not continue to approve of each other, conflicts seldom can be resolved.

Parents who fear circumstances such as cohabitation, homosexual behavior, cults, and drug use have great difficulty developing the perspective that their NQA's are moving into adulthood and, therefore, must take the major share of responsibility for their own behavior. In discussing control and authority in Chapter 2, we spoke of the developing autonomy of children during the NQA years. During one class session with parents, after saying that it was necessary for parents to push the birds out of the nest so they could learn to fly on their own, from the back of the room one of the fathers responded in a deep voice. "Yeah, and sometimes the cat gets them." Nevertheless, most birds fly, and on their own, not attached to their parents. Letting go and getting free involves risks, but, even in the fearful area of conflicts in life-style, risks can be minimal if parents and NQA's remember that each can still respect the other even while feeling free to disagree with the behavior of the other.

Parents and NQA's should not lay the responsibility for their behavior on the other like a game of pin the tail on the donkey. They should maintain contact with each other even when the most serious conflicts arise. They should minimize attempts at coercion, harping, carping, and hand-wringing. Both should keep in mind the resiliency of the family and its members. Even as NQA's behave in ways often irritating to their parents, as they grow older they almost always adopt life-styles more similar to that of the parents than to any other group with which they may have contact.

And that should be a comfort.

REFERENCES

[1] *The Milwaukee Journal*, February 9, 1977, p. 20.
[2] A. Kinsey, and others, *Sexual Behavior in the Human Male* (Philadelphia: W.B. Saunders, 1948), Chap. 21.
[3] D. Black, "Why Kids Join Cults," *Woman's Day* (February 1977), p. 166.

FOR ADDITIONAL READING

MEDVED, M., and D. WALLECHINSKY, *What Really Happened to the Class of '65?* New York: Ballantine Books, 1976.
    Biographies of the NQA years, the groups, life-styles, problems, conflicts that are experienced and explored as the class of '65 achieves adulthood.

Cohabitation

KING, M., *Cohabitation Handbook, Living Together and the Law*. Berkeley, Calif.: Ten Speed Press, 1975.

Description of some legal problems that can complicate a living-together arrangement, with suggestions to avoid pitfalls. Don't be put off by the illustrations; for information is relevant and useful.

Drugs

BRECHER, E., and the EDITORS of CONSUMER REPORTS, *Licit and Illicit Drugs*. Mt. Vernon, N.Y.: Consumers Union, 1972.

This book covers the field better than any other. Should be required reading for all parents and NQA's.

Cults

The popular magazines offer some of the best material on cults. There are also some good books on the subject.

BLACK, D., "Why Kids Join Cults" *Woman's Day* (February, 1977).

DANER, F. J., *American Children of KRSNA*. New York: Holt, Rinehart & Winston, 1976.

A scholarly book on the Hare Krishna movement. Might be a little hard to read, but offers interesting insights on why young people join cults.

RASSMUSSEN, M., "How Sun Myung Moon Lures America's Children," *McCalls* (September 1976).

RICE, B., "Honor Thy Father Moon," *Psychology Today* (January 1976).

ROTHCHILD, J., and W.S. ROTHCHILD, *The Children of the Counterculture*. Garden City, N.Y.: Doubleday, 1976.

Excellent book on communes and the children who live in them. Includes a description of a school run by Hare Krishnas for their children.

SAGE, W., "The War on the Cults," *Human Behavior* (October 1976).

Homosexuality

FAIRCHILD, BETTY, *Parents of Gays*.

A privately published booklet, which lists names and addresses where help can be found. To obtain a copy write Lambda Rising, 1724 20th St., N.W., Washington, D.C. 20009.

HOBSON, L.Z., *Consenting Adult*. Garden City, N.Y.: Doubleday, 1975.

Fictional account of a son's revelation of his homosexuality to his family.

WEINBERG, G., *Society and the Healthy Homosexual*. New York: Anchor Books, 1972.

Discusses stereotypes and myths of homosexuality, how to tell parents. Useful for both parents and NQA's.

WYDEN, P., and B. WYDEN, *Growing Up Straight: What Every Thoughtful Parent Should Know About Homosexuality*. New York: Stein and Day, 1977.

Discusses the influence that parents have in the development of homosexuality in their children.

Hazards
to
Personal
Functioning

There are hazards to personal functioning that get in the way during the NQA years. Some call these "coping problems," others name them "ego problems." However they may be labeled, these hazards affect an individual's ability to grow to adulthood. There is a big difference between the issues raised in the chapter on life-styles and the ones we will now discuss. This chapter focuses less on what NQA's may want to do and more on what they should be able to do. The issues arise around definition and self-concept. Often some kind of action on the part of the parent is necessary.

The most common hazards to personal functioning are:

1. *Alienation.* ("I won't have anything to do with you and all you stand for anymore, ever!")
2. *Illness.* ("I'm really not quite well enough to face up to the demands made upon me.")
3. *Anxiety.* ("I'm too scared to take that exam, go out with that person, apply for that job.")
4. *Depression.* The most common of all the hazards. ("Why bother? Nobody cares about me! And that's no wonder because I'm no good anyway! A terrible person! What the hell's the use? Everything I do is wrong!")
5. *Suicide.* An extension of either alienation or depression. (It is possible for suicide to be an issue of power. NQA's sometimes use the threat of suicide to control their par-

ents. In such a case, the threat should not be seen as a sign of inability to cope with the demands of life. We will return to this later.)

In common usage these terms denote mental illness, implying a breakdown in either the ability to function or to see the world realistically. But we use these terms here to describe hazards which set up roadblocks to the achievement of maturity and independence. Nevertheless, parents are often advised to deal with them as though they were illnesses. See the doctor. Get treatment. Whether something is defined as a hazard or as a mental illness is all important, *for the definition of what is going on determines the behavior that follows.*

Erik Erikson is a famous popularizer of the "medical model" approach to human behavior, although he probably didn't set out to be. It is his idea that life consists of a series of crises, each one to be resolved before one can go on to the next. The life crisis that youths face is that of finding their identity.[1] This has come to be called the "identity crisis."

Erikson was referring to sexual identity, and most of his writings were about males. He says that individuals have certain tasks to accomplish during this period, and, if they do not, problems may be anticipated at later stages of development.

It is interesting that although Erikson divided life into eight crises to be resolved during a lifetime, only one has caught the popular fancy. One never hears of a person suffering from a "generativity" crisis" (the seventh stage), or an "autonomy crisis" (the second stage), or, for that matter, any of the others. Therapists, on the other hand, frequently diagnose persons in the NQA age range as experiencing an "identity crisis," as though this was the reason for every problem from suicide to drug abuse.

Even Erikson himself became worried about the way his theory had become fashionable. In a later work,[2] he wondered: "Would some of our youth act so openly confused and confusing if they did not *know* they were *supposed* to have an identity crisis?" (Erikson's italics)

A number of theorists have taken the view that disturbance during this period is so usual that if a young person has an *unruffled* life during this time, there is reason for concern. Anna Freud, in talking about "good" children, felt that they were "perhaps more than any others, in need of therapeutic help to remove the inner restrictions and clear the path for normal development, however "upsetting" the latter may prove to be".[3] Others agree that upheaval, unhappiness, and personal uncertainty are the norm.[4]

Parents who get along well with their children might be left wondering just where they have gone wrong. According to this line of reasoning, sickness is health, abnormal is normal, and so on. This could be dismissed as nonsense, if it weren't taken so seriously by so many. The problem for families is that these theories mingle in popular thought. The combination leaves parents feeling incompetent to handle their children when things are going well, and implies that when things are not going well, treatment is needed.

Another kind of advice that is given to parents is that they should become therapists themselves and use therapeutic techniques on their children. Parents are told to treat the children as though they were their patients rather than their sons and daughters.

An example of parents as therapists is contained in the book *P.E.T., Parent Effectiveness Training* by Thomas Gordon.[5] This is a popularization of the nondirective counseling methods originated by Carl Rogers. It is based on the philosophy that people are all born good, but they are later corrupted by society and its agents (for instance, parents). In this system of therapy, the therapist tries to stand out of a patient's way so that he or she can become completely herself or himself. . . Essential goodness will shine through if it is allowed to do so. As a system of therapy, this has many advocates.

As a system of parenting, however, it presents problems. In therapy, one is supposed to do one's best to remain objective and to avoid identifying with the patient. A therapist is not supposed to become emotionally involved with the client. However, parents cannot avoid being emotionally involved with their children. Most NQA's do not need therapy, but if they do, *parents should not be the ones to provide it.* Even psychologists and psychiatrists do not attempt to treat members of their own families.

Parents have socializing and nurturing responsibilities in raising children. They provide their children with solutions to problems that come from interaction with others. These solutions vary greatly depending on the parents' background or culture, the area of the country in which they live, or the type of parenting parents themselves experienced. Parents interpret society to their children. They also identify with their children and are sympathetic to their problems and needs. All families provide some sort of framework within which the individual relates to those with whom he or she comes into contact.

During the NQA period, this framework of patterns of behavior, which was anchored around the home, is modified. The NQA is being pushed out of the familiar setting bit by bit. NQA's have to learn to adapt to new ways of behaving that are oriented around work, college and dormitory, military service, all that we call "being on one's own." Parents are no longer able to provide the same kind of support they provided earlier. They are not as close at hand, and other groups to which the NQA's belong are becoming more important. These other reference groups will relate to the NQA in ways that are different from the ways used by the parents. Whether they are more kindly or more critical is not the important point. What is important is that they are different, unfamiliar, and strange, and, therefore, situations arise in which the

NQA feels stress. All NQA's run into this. . . . some feel it more deeply than others. Those who do may react in one of the ways we call hazards.

Those who downgrade the importance of the family during this period neglect the most significant resource available for minimizing the hazards. In fact, the family is at times the *only* resource available to the NQA. Parents should recognize that they are competent to contribute, and NQA's should recognize that their parents' usefulness is not limited to the provision of material resources.

When hazards to personal performance arise, NQA's do not usually need treatment. But they do need their parents. The family is their original reference group. Parents can be either helpful or hindering forces as the NQA struggles to learn to behave in ways that will enable him or her to become accepted in other adult reference groups. Parents are called upon to use nurturing skills to help NQA's regain the feeling that they are worthy, and parents must also encourage their children to go out and try again. They must make suggestions as to how success might be more possible on the next attempt.

Since the NQA period is relatively new, parents are often unsure of themselves. They worry that they have no guidelines to fall back on. In fact, they do have guidelines— the fundamentals of the relationship between them and the NQA remains the same. Only the specifics change to reflect the change in expectations of society and the parents toward the NQA. Parents can be confident that what has gone on before in the family has built a foundation from which the present situation can be handled.

This discussion of hazards to personal functioning is organized around the single issue of relationships with peers (mostly of the opposite sex) to show that it is possible for a variety of reactions to take place in response to similar sets of circumstances. There is not a direct one-to-one response wherein a certain button is pushed and out comes, for instance, alienation. Human behavior is never so simple.

We spoke of the complicated nature of human behavior in Chapter 1, how individual behavior is channeled into certain streams of possibilities that are set by the social order. Within those possibilities, individual influences are brought to bear on behavior by the interaction of persons who are important to each other. Parents and NQA's are very important to each other.

In the illustrations that follow, nonfamily influences that interact with the NQA (school, church, peers, and so on) are downplayed because this is a book about relationships between parents and their "not quite adult" children. Even when these other factors are excluded, the finger of blame is not pointed at the parents for all the problems an NQA experiences. The point is that regardless of how a hazard originates, it is possible for parents to assist NQA's to work their way out and move toward maturity.

Before the NQA period rolls around, young people have certainly had some relationships with the opposite sex. These are fairly routine—home, school, community, and peer group settings. They may seem to be permanent and stable, but with the change in setting required by moving out of the home, graduating from high school, having friends scatter from familiar haunts and leaving the community, these routine relationships are upset, and others must take their place. When routine patterns must be replaced by new ones, anxiety is heightened, mistakes are made, and doubt can arise about one's ability to proceed.

To whom have NQA's gone in the past for advice? The only persons consistently available are the parents. Teachers change, friends and neighbors move away, ministers and priests accept calls to other parishes, grandparents move to Florida. Parents are available and hope to be consulted, but if they see the issues only from the standpoint of the dangers they were warned about in their youth, they will cut off the discussion of the many possibilities that openly exist today. When NQA's feel that it is impossible for them to discuss the complete range of choices available to them with their parents, they have less opportunity to figure out the advantages or disadvantages of the choices and to see what these might mean for their future.

What is a socially acceptable partner? Why? What about cohabitation? What is homosexuality? How important is virginity? What about playing the field? What is the danger of VD? Can this be minimized? What is birth control? How do the various methods work? Will an unmarried pregnancy ruin your life? Is that better or worse than forced marriage? Or an abortion? Is divorce the end of one's value as a human being? Is an extravagant marriage ceremony important? Should one try to marry young or wait till one is older? Can one balance marriage, children, schooling, a career? What about meaningful relationships outside of one's social, ethnic, or religious background? And, most important, if one makes a bad choice about any of these things, is life finished? These are all questions young people want to talk about.

NQA's who have no one with whom to discuss these issues, *from the idealistic, risk-taking viewpoint of the NQA*, will find it difficult to make an effective choice. In fact, they may be unable to choose at all. They either wander into situations randomly or become unable to participate in anything. Some persons feel that they are actually given no chance to choose since all possibilities seem bad or dangerous. When an individual is presented with a series of negative choices, alienation is often the result.

Parents do not realize that they sometimes present only negative choices. They will say that there is little communication between them and their NQA's, but they do not realize that communication is more than direct conversation about a specific issue. Parents often express opinions that are not directed to their children but are overheard by them and incorporated into their thinking. Many studies have shown that NQA's tend to adopt most of the values of their parents even though they may reject or question specific items.[6]

Alienation

Alienation is withdrawal from relationships with people or groups because the relationship has become unsatisfying to the individual. Alienation often comes about as a result of the individual's inability to pick a satisfying course of action from the many available choices. All may offer some possibility of satisfaction, but all also offer great uncertainty and, therefore, produce fear.

Maggie is an example of alienation. She had always been close to her parents. They felt that they had openly discussed her concerns, but, in fact, at the age of 18, Maggie had seen more of life than her parents knew about. Some of her high school acquaintances were going through divorces. She knew girls who were unwed mothers and two who had had abortions. Although Maggie knew a lot about the kinds of problems that sex could cause, her actual experience was limited. She had dated often and had enjoyed heavy petting, but she was a virgin. She wanted to have sexual relations both to satisfy her curiosity and because she felt she was missing an important experience, but she was frightened. She didn't want to get married because of the divorces she had witnessed among her contemporaries. Besides, her parents frequently emphasized how important it was to avoid being tied down by family responsibilities before "she was ready." Maggie thought her parents must use some form of birth control because she had put together her parents' ages and the age of their youngest child. However, in common with many young people her age, Maggie did not like to think that her parents enjoyed sexual activity. In her opinion, they might possibly have intercourse three or four times a year, but only in the most prosaic fashion. She was sure they knew nothing about the things she wanted to ask about, things like oral sex and what forms of birth control are effective and was it perverted to have sex in odd positions in strange places. Her parents often discussed the negative aspects of sex but never their own sexuality, so Maggie did not see them as a potential source of information.

Maggie had heard her parents' comments on a local girl who openly admitted having an abortion. This girl, they said, would never recover from the guilt feelings. Of course, they said that another girl who had had a baby out of wedlock and gave it up for adoption would always wonder what had become of it and would never recover from the guilt feelings. In the meantime, the sale of contraceptives to young people was terribly wrong. To Maggie's mind, there was nothing left to discuss. All avenues were closed. She was too young to be "tied down" by marriage, and nothing else would do.

Although Maggie accepted the majority of her parents' opinions, she had several friends who were living with boys, and this made sense to her. Maggie wanted to find out if she was ready for marriage, but if she was wrong she wanted to avoid the trauma of divorce. She knew her parents would object, so when she met a seemingly knowledgeable boy she thought she liked, she made a decision without her parents' aid. In fact, she arranged things so that they would not know about her great experiment. She took off, leaving a note saying that her parents should not worry; she was going out of town for a few weeks and would get in touch with them soon.

Her parents reacted in a fashion other parents would not find too surprising. They panicked. They called Maggie's friends to ask if they knew where she had gone. They did not. They went to the office where she worked and discovered that she had manufactured a story about an illness and had taken an indefinite sick leave. When her employers found out that she was not sick, they changed her status to unemployed. Maggie's parents called the police and requested they put out an all-points bulletin. Soon Maggie's picture appeared in the newspaper and on TV as a missing person (last seen wearing blue jeans, and so on). The parents discussed the problem with their minister.

Meanwhile, Maggie was being introduced to the counter-culture. She did not like it at all, for she had not rejected her parents' values.

Shortly she called home, and her parents again reacted in a not unusual fashion. They scolded her for all the pain she had caused them and told her about how they had contacted her friends, her employers, and the police. Maggie was horrified and embarrassed. She had laid her plans so that she could go away and return if she chose without anyone knowing what she was doing, and her parents had apparently told everyone in town. Furthermore, in expressing their concern for her well-being, they asked questions like, "Are you sure you aren't pregnant?" Maggie didn't think so, but, in fact, she wasn't really sure. Although she had called to say she wanted to come home, she decided it was impossible to return to her former life and that her only choice was to stay with her new group. She is now drifting aimlessly, taking drugs, living with different boys, and affecting the jargon of her group. "Society is too messed up" for her to want to participate in it.

Maggie's parents cannot imagine why their daughter changed so drastically. She calls home every few weeks and they always ask her "Why." She has no answer, and their telephone conversations usually end in arguments. The contacts are becoming less frequent.

Some people deliberately choose the kind of life Maggie was leading, and they are successful in it. Most do not deliberately choose, and Maggie is one of those. Since her boy friend took off with another woman, she has not been able to enjoy the open, casual relationships with both sexes that are available. She is bitter about her parents, who seem to have cut off all avenues of escape from a life she does not like. She has lost her ability to function effectively, to change her situation. All she can see is a series of negative choices. She suffers periods of depression and has considered suicide.

Maggie is exhibiting many of the signs of alienation. There are other courses of action she might have taken rather than running away with her boy friend. But let's leave Maggie for the moment and talk about a young man who ran into a very different hazard.

Illness

Jack was a handsome young man and very popular with the girls. He had strong sexual desires, but he did not feel comfortable discussing sex with his traditionally minded parents. Jack's mother had warned him repeatedly of the dangers of contacting VD and of the possibility of being lured into a bad marriage by a wily female who might deliberately allow herself to get pregnant. His father had spoken of dire results of "too much" masturbation. In common with Maggie, Jack had never heard his parents talk of their own sexuality. Other information Jack had received from his peers, and a wide variety of reading matter ranging from the Bible to *Playboy* magazine, had not assisted him in defining the elements he wished to resolve in his personal situation. By putting together the information received from his parents, the Bible, and *Playboy*, he had come to the conclusion that sex caused problems for almost everybody.

Away at college, he met a girl who had drawn quite a different set of conclusions from very similar information. She encouraged Jack, and they became intimate. Jack enjoyed the relationship, but he worried about his mother's advice on "wily females." He tried to stay away from his girlfriend, but that produced worries about how much was "too much" masturbation. Soon Jack began to have severe abdominal pains. They became so bad that he found it necessary to drop out of college and return home.

He found that he could avoid the pain as long as he remained at home and did not date. Jack and his parents have, as yet, made no connection between Jack's physical discomfort and his difficulties in resolving his questions about sex. At this point, it is possible that the situation could be reordered, but if illness should become a set pattern of his life, Jack may never move out of the NQA period.

Jack was offered a series of negative choices, and he took refuge in illness. Like Maggie, he suffers from depression and has considered suicide. It is possible to substitute Maggie for Jack and Jack for Maggie. Maggie could have just as well become ill. Equally, Jack might have been the one to run away with a girlfriend.

Anxiety

Anxiety is different. It is produced less by guilt and more by fear. It is sometimes known as the "sweats" by the young persons who have experienced this discomfort.

All the hazards we are discussing have some fear connected with them, but the feelings commonly called anxiety are marked off from others because they are less likely to result in depression or alienation. Anxiety is signified by agitation, sweating, expressions of fear, and an inability to perform in the situation that produces the fear.

Alonzo's mother and father divorced when Alonzo was 10. His mother remarried when he was in his midteens.

Alonzo sees his natural father infrequently, but he knows him to be a charming chauvinist who is preoccupied with his sexual prowess—one who considers women to be useful only as a sexual outlet for men.

Alonzo's stepfather is kind and loving to his mother, but he does not discuss the relationship with Alonzo. Alonzo's mother believes that a divorced parent should not "cut down" the absent parent in the presence of the children. She avoids any discussion of merits or faults of Alonzo's father. She has effectively put behind her the traumatic period during which the divorce took place, but Alonzo has found this more difficult to do. He does not like his natural father, whom he resembles in many ways. And it is obvious, even though she refuses to discuss it, that his mother did not like his father either—hence, the divorce. She has never explained why. Alonzo regards his stepfather as a person to look up to. But since the stepfather does not brag about his sexual encounters in the way his natural father did, Alonzo is mystified about his stepfather's sexual attitudes.

Alonzo's tentative explorations in the uncharted areas of sexual relationships in high school were unsatisfying and confusing. Reading about sex in magazines had confirmed what his natural father had told him. The only reason to know a girl was to get her in bed as soon as possible. A really super girl would beat him to the mattress. On one hand, he wanted the friendly loving relationship that he could see existed between his mother and stepfather, but, on the other, he found it easier to react as his natural father had. Was it possible to have a good relationship that included sex, or were the two mutually antagonistic?

Alonzo became more and more confused about how to behave with young women. He went to prostitutes, thinking that might help, but he found that he was unable to have an erection. He discovered that other women now also produced this reaction. The more he tried, the more anxious he became and the more failure he experienced.

Alonzo's confusion and his lack of success with girls, who seemed attracted to him, made him so uncomfortable that he began to avoid girls whenever he could. In their presence, he became fidgety and sweated profusely because he could find no way to suppress his desires or to satisfy them.

Alonzo has become more and more of a loner, even at the factory where he works. He has begun to establish a ritual that provides safety. Every morning, he arises early and runs several miles. Then he goes to work. He always takes a sandwich so he will not have to go to the lunchroom where the secretaries eat. He works hard, comes home, eats dinner with his mother and stepfather, and then goes to a local bar frequented by men. He drinks a few beers, comes home about eleven, and goes to bed. On weekends he sleeps late, does an occasional odd job for his mother, and goes to the bar. Since he sees few women, he keeps his anxiety under control.

Although in many ways Alonzo is a model son, his mother and stepfather are worried about him. They realize he is cutting himself off from most of his former friends and that he has stopped dating. They don't think he is very happy, and they are worried about his lack of ambition. They talk a lot to each other about their concern, but they have not tried to talk to Alonzo.

Alonzo's natural father has long since diagnosed the problem. "Alonzo," he says, "must be a 'queer.' His mother made him that way."

Alonzo is definitely not a homosexual, nor does he suffer guilt feelings about sex. His anxiety is the result of confusion about the roles of the two men who are closest to him—one who does not talk and the other who talks too much.

Alonzo might have chosen instead to move into a structured situation, such as one of the religious sects that presently flourish, or he might have gotten ill as Jack did.

Depression

Depression is the emotional "common cold" of our society, and NQA's are as susceptible as anyone else.

We are constantly bombarded with the need to be successful, more successful than our parents, our neighbors, our friends. We are told that success can be instantaneous if we just go at it right. The proper toothpaste produces instant whiteness and assures popularity. The proper breakfast cereal produces instant health and strength. The proper makeup produces instant loveliness. The proper finance company provides ready cash when you need it. The proper credit card assures instant status worldwide.

Unfortunately, life seldom works out so well. Toothaches arrive and relationships fail regardless of the tooth-paste used. Exercise is needed no matter what one eats for breakfast. Makeup helps some people, but, often as not, your skin breaks out. Finance companies are not generous parental substitutes. They insist on being paid back on time and they charge high interest. Right and justice do not always triumph. Expectations must be scaled down.

Parents have experienced the painful reactions that occur when one is forced to relinquish a myth or one discovers one's inability to realize an expectation. With the passage of time, most were able to work their way out of this kind of pain. NQA's are in the process of learning which of their many expectations are realistic for them and which must be discarded or reworked. Some become overwhelmed when they find out that they must put aside popular myths for realism. NQA's often suffer periods of depression . . . so often, in fact, that is the reason depression is said to be as common as the common cold.

Cherie is one such NQA. Her parent's thought she was one of the nicest, smartest, prettiest girls imaginable. They expected great things from her, and in high school she did not disappoint them. She got good grades, made the pom-pom squad, won a good part in the class play, dated a succession of "nice" boys, had a good time, and stayed out of trouble. On occasion Cherie and her parents argued, but the issues were resolved with only minor turmoil. Cherie respected her parents and accepted their values. She also accepted their assessment of her and had no doubts that she would easily fulfill all their expectations. These included graduation from college, working at an interesting career for a bit, and then giving it up to marry a nice young man and living happily ever after. After all, was she not the prettiest, nicest, smartest girl imaginable?

Neither Cherie nor her parents realized that her social success in high school was based to a large degree on the family's position in the community and the parents' indulgence and manipulation ("They were only trying to help"). For instance, Cherie's parents had bought their house because it was such a nice place for young people to come to. The pool table and the ping-pong table and the ready supply of soft drinks and potato chips assured that the crowd met there. Cherie's parents always could be counted on for rides to anywhere. Cherie's mother helped with her class work. Mother typed her papers and corrected spelling and punctuation as she went along. Cherie wore the latest clothes and went regularly to the beauty parlor. Her Mom and Dad never missed a meeting of the PTA, a play performance, a ball game, or anything that involved Cherie.

There was always so much going on. Cherie grew convinced that this activity, which was as much the result of her parents' efforts as her own, was a sign of her own success with her girl friends, her teachers, and, most of all, with boys. She was a "popular" girl.

After high school graduation, Cherie's parents sent her to an expensive college several hundred miles away from home. For the first time in her life, Cherie was competing with her peers without close parental support. Much to Cherie's surprise, she turned out to be average, at least in comparison with her classmates. Many were prettier, smarter, nicer, or more popular, and some seemed to be all of these put together. It was, after all, a very good school.

In high school, Cherie had made nearly a straight "A" average. In college, she found she was having trouble maintaining a low "B" average. The "best" sorority did not invite her to join, although she did get bids to two others. She dated

some freshman boys, but she did not realize that it was necessary to reestablish her reputation as a "nice" girl. She did not
know how to handle their aggressive approach. The desirable
junior and senior boys ignored her. Her English teacher, a
handsome young man whom Cherie thought was quite fond of
her, gave her a "D" on an important paper. When the sorority
pledge dance came along, Cherie was supposed to ask a boy.
She asked four and received four turn downs—all had acceptable reasons, but to Cherie it was a sign of her lack of personal
attractiveness. The one boy who did show interest in Cherie
was termed "not good enough for her" by Cherie's parents
when she brought the boy home to visit. Couldn't she do any
better, they asked?

During her freshman year Cherie experienced no
dramatic failures, or at least none that would be apparent to
the casual observer. If "average" was considered acceptable,
Cherie did fine. Unfortunately, neither Cherie's expectations
nor those of her parents were pitched at that level. Her parents continually urged her to try harder, but she was doing
the best she could.

Her grades got progressively worse, and she finished the
year with several deficiencies. She refused to return the following year. She wanted to stay home and work for a while,
she said. She applied for several jobs and was turned down.
She stopped applying.

Cherie constantly went over the events of her year at
school, endlessly talking about where she had gone wrong.
Everything must have been her fault, she said. She com-
plained of being tired all the time, but she had difficulty sleep-
ing. She found no pleasure in seeing her old friends or in
participating in the many activities she had formerly enjoyed.
For instance, although she had liked making some of her own
clothing, she now refused to sew. When her mother took her
to a fabric store, Cherie could not decide on a pattern or
material.

Although Cherie had always been healthy, she was now

troubled by assorted stomachaches and chest pains. She became irritable and annoyed at her parents' slightest suggestions. Now she mostly keeps to herself, sleeps late, and watches television.

Cherie is exhibiting many of the signs of depression, and her parents are worried sick about her. She might also have reacted to her problems in the same ways as Jack, Maggie, and Alonzo reacted to theirs.

Suicide

Suicide is the ultimate expression of alienation and depression. The word strikes fear into the hearts of most everyone, and certainly parents.

Small wonder too. Newspapers and magazines constantly remind readers that suicide is the second leading cause of death for persons in the NQA age range. The suicide rate in this age group has risen enormously, they say, perhaps even doubled in the past few years. These articles are frightening for they focus attention on scary statistics without relating them to the overall picture.

As we have said before, as a group, NQA's are very healthy. Their death rate from disease and illness is lower than for people of any other age range.[7] This is why accidents and suicides rank as the first and second causes of death. The actual figures are low compared with the number of suicides that take place in the rest of the population. The rate of suicide in the 25–44 age group is higher, as are the actual number of deaths by suicide. The rate is still higher in the 45–64 range and highest of all in the group over age 64. NQA's are less likely to die by suicide than their parents or grandparents.[8]

However, the suicide of a parent is not generally considered to be something the child should or could have prevented. A parent whose child commits suicide feels not only the loss of someone close, but also great guilt. Parents are often made to feel that if only the right thing had been done at the right time, the parent could have prevented the tragic loss. This view does not take into consideration the many factors that contribute to the individual's decision to end it all, factors beyond parental control.

NQA's are in the process of realizing that they are responsible for their own lives. When one takes responsibility for one's own life, one realizes that the option exists for ending it if one chooses. In the struggle for control of their lives, NQA's discover that they possess within themselves the possibility for ultimate control. They like to discuss suicide because they are developing their own philosophy of life, their own moral values. They spend a lot of time talking about whether something is right or wrong, and whether something else is more right or more wrong. For instance, they might ask if a person would be more right to fight and kill in a war or to commit suicide. Parents who are painfully aware of the scary headlines and statistics find it hard to distinguish between a philosophical discussion of suicide and a serious threat.

Some NQA's use suicide threats as a means to control not only their own lives, but also the lives and resources of their parents. Often we hear of parents who control children by having "a condition" that flares up whenever they are crossed. The reverse—the young person who threatens self-destruction to get his or her own way—is seldom mentioned.

A mistaken belief that contributes to parents' fear is that suicide is always a symptom of mental illness. This illness, people think, affects not only the individual but the entire family. Studies have shown that this is true in only a small proportion of cases. Suicides are most likely to be caused by disturbances in relationships with others, usually members of the opposite sex. On rare occasions, the disturbance in relationship is within the family.[9]

When a young person begins to talk about suicide, parents are faced with making logical judgments about an emotional issue. It is not easy to do. But after the shock wears off, and normal thought processes have been reinstituted, parents should try to think through just what is going on. They will want to try to figure out what has prompted the statement. If it is related to a specific matter, such as living or not living at home, the use of a car or going on a trip, or in some other area where the NQA wants a material advantage, there is little likelihood that the young person is seriously planning to carry out the threat. Parents can treat this as they would any of the other challenges that NQA's throw at them. When the NQA realizes that this most final and dramatic presentation does not yield the hoped for result, he or she will stop using this type of behavior and grow a bit more toward adulthood. This type of threat is usually stated in "If you don't, I'll. . ." terms.

The philosophical musings may or may not be more serious. If the NQA is enjoying life and now showing other signs of alienation or depression, parents can offer their opinions and listen to the NQA's without worrying too much. NQA's ask about a lot of things because they want to know what parents think. They are quite capable of asking how one feels about suicide and the latest Woody Allen movie in the same breath.

If the talk of suicide comes as a result of some disruption in relationships with others whom the NQA feels are important (whether or not the parents agree), or if the young person is suffering from alienation or depression, and if the threat is generalized—not related to a specific issue—there is cause for concern.

This is a time when parents may want to seek specialized assistance. There are, in most metropolitan centers, either parent's helplines or suicide hotlines. Talking the problem over can help parents to clarify their own thinking about what is going on. Dealing with a person who is entertaining thoughts of suicide is not something with which most people have experience. Professionals do, and this is the time to take advantage of it. However, parents cannot just dump the problem onto the professional. They can use them to learn ways to be of greater assistance to the NQA who is asking for help. Sometimes treatment is needed, and, if so, parents must actively participate. They should also try to maintain a calm, positive attitude toward life.

No one—friend, NQA, parent, or therapist—should ever say that a person with suicidal thoughts is "sick" or "crazy." Such labeling just increases the feelings of worthlessness that have brought on the thoughts of suicide in the first place.

If a suicide does occur, parents may want to get some counselling to help them cope with their loss and to sort out their feelings and emotions. But it is well to remember that the chances of an NQA suicide are far less than the headlines would lead one to believe.

Minimizing Hazards

Let's return to Maggie, Jack, Alonzo, and Cherie. They are suffering assorted hazards and are turning to their parents for assistance. None is saying, "I'm sick, so I need help." Three of them are staying at home when they should be with their peers. They are worrying their parents by their lack of independence, their inability to let go and get free. Maggie calls home frequently in spite of the arguments, and her parents send her money from time to time. She is alienated from her former life and would like to have her parents help to return to it.

In these illustrations, a common factor is the lack of a two-way discussion. The parents want to be of assistance, and the NQA's need that assistance, but there has been no consistent effort on the part of the parents or the NQA's to talk or to listen to each other. The conversations that take place resemble an athletic contest where the number of points scored determines the winner; and as in any contest where there is a winner, there is also a loser. Since nobody likes to lose all the time, the loser gives up and stops talking. Oddly enough, in parent–NQA relationships, both sides usually feel like the loser in the arguments and so both give up talking to each other. "Well, I just can't communicate with Dad and Mom," they say. Or, "I can't talk to my kids!"

It is important to continue to talk and to listen to each other. When a young person is suffering through a hazard, it is particularly important for the parents to forget about winning or losing and concentrate on keeping up a productive conversation.

Parents should talk to others outside the immediate family too. The problems we are discussing are not unique, but all too often families assume that they are the only ones who have been so afflicted. In classes with parents, the authors were surprised at the constant repetition of phrases such as "We are so glad to find that we are not alone" or "We thought we were the only ones." By talking with others, parents can learn new ways to resolve issues. They may come up with a variety of good solutions since, in helping another person, one may have to try a lot of different things.

It is rather like finding a way through a maze. You head off confidently expecting to go directly to the center and find yourself bumping into walls in a series of dead-end streets. Then you have to backtrack and set off on a new course. If you keep at it and avoid going down the same blind alley over and over again, eventually you get to where you wanted to go. Unfortunately, in relationships, the tendency is to go over the same ground rather than seeking new directions.

Human beings use talk to resolve the problematic nature of situations. Routine situations require little talk since it is clear what is expected and what should be done. Dad sits in this chair, Mom sits in that one. Please turn off the light in your room. What's good on television tonight? That was a good dinner. And, it's little Susie's turn to do the dishes. One doesn't have to think too much because most of what goes on is automatic.

For NQA's many situations are not routine, and responses cannot be automatic. They have to function in new ways to meet new demands. Much more talk than usual is necessary. The NQA's and parents in the illustrations given earlier did not make any consistent effort to understand their problems, to see what might lie behind them, or to look for new ways to get things in hand.

The parents, who have been through the NQA years, tend to assume that they know exactly what problems will occur in the life of the NQA. So they do not make an effort to listen and learn from the young person what he or she is really feeling or to find out what he or she is really worrying about. NQA's consider their parents out-of-date, but they have not tried to find out if the parents have anything to offer. The conversation has stopped and the hazards grow. And the possibility of eventual breakdown in function becomes great.

Maggie's parents talk to her every week or so, but they express their worries rather than listening to hers. She would like to come home, but she feels that path is blocked to her. She wants some help in extricating herself from an undesirable situation, yet her parents' fears for her prevent discussion of other options. She always has to justify what she did to them, rather than being able to say, "Look, folks, I blew it. Help me."

Maggie and her parents are stuck in a blind alley and are not yet seeking a new path. Her parents might suggest that she go to school some place for a while, visit an aunt, live with friends in another city. Maggie could think about coming home and not worrying about her big "mistake." A lot of her friends and acquaintances had made much more damaging ones.

Maggie and her parents are caught in a time warp. They

are not paying attention to the past or the future, only to the present. Maggie's dramatic exit from home is actually an event that happened in the past. It's over, but, to this family, it is being relived and revived in the present. They are looking neither to the good relationship they had enjoyed in the past nor using the present to seek solutions they can make happen in the future. They spend their present worrying about a small slice of the past, focusing on a cross section of time rather than trying to gain perspective by taking a longitudinal view.

However, there is one bright spot. They are still talking, and talk makes new choices possible.

Jack and his parents are stuck in another type of blind alley. They started down the same road as did Maggie's family, but they got lost because they have neglected to look at the map.

Questions about relationships with the opposite sex need to be answered, especially during the NQA years. Parents should be able to anticipate this and prepare themselves to answer. Sometimes the questions are asked by actions rather than by words, and it becomes the parents' task to interpret what is going on. This interpreting is a continuance of the socializing and nurturing functions of the family. It assumes great importance when hazards arise.

Knowledge can be gained from many sources. There are a multitude of books on the market. At the end of this chapter, some books are listed that might be helpful.

Professionals can be consulted. They are a good source of information about ways of improving relationships. The problem here is that unless parents have some prior knowledge, they may find themselves confused by the professionals. The helping professions are not standardized. The type of knowledge imparted is based largely on the professional's own personal philosophy.

A person who asks five different medical doctors the

same question will often come up with more than one answer. "Yes, you should have that operation immediately." "No, it won't hurt if you wait till next year." There is some disagreement, but there is far more agreement.

If you ask a question of five different members of helping professions, you can easily get five (sometimes six or seven) completely different answers, depending on the orientation of the particular profession. A psychiatrist who follows the teachings of Sigmund Freud will suggest a very different course of action from a psychologist who believes in transactional analysis or one who uses biofeedback. A behaviorist is as far away in thinking from a Rogerian as the north pole is from the south. There are psychologists, psychiatrists, social workers, guidance counselors, ministers—and any one of these may use any of the different treatment philosophies. There is also a sprinkling of just plain "quacks."

Licensing procedures vary from state to state. In most cases, licensing gives individuals the right to call themselves a certain type of counselor, but it never prevents people from manufacturing a new type of title and hanging out their shingles. People who consult with others should make sure of two things. One is that the helper is truly a professional, and the other is that the philosophy espoused is not too far removed from that of the family's philosophy.

Much knowledge has been obtained about human relationships in the last 20 or so years. Professionals have access to this knowledge and can help people to see things in new ways.

Young people bring home a great deal of information. This source of knowledge should not be rejected simply because what they say is new or different. Most children are more into contemporary life and thought than are their parents. They see things from a different viewpoint and describe what they see in a different language. Young people are inclined to be more concerned with feelings, while parents are worrying about outward appearances. Both can learn from each other, and, in so doing, achieve a better balance between the two.

It is part of the socializing and nurturing functions for the parents to integrate all these sources of knowledge with their own wisdom acquired from years of experience. Then they will be ready to provide guidance to their NQA's who need assistance in making choices among the possible courses of action open to them.

Jack's parents could have been more helpful to him if they had *known* that some of his difficulties could be related to what they told him in the past. If they had known that their present knowledge was limited and out-of-date, they also might have realized that it was not useful to Jack. If Jack's family could have discussed relationships in ways other than merely citing pitfalls to avoid, Jack would have had a different perspective on his situation. Jack's parents might also have found out that physical pain can be related to a stressful situation like the one in which Jack found himself.

Jack's parents were trying to get through a maze by following a map given to them by *their* parents. They are under the impression that the maze remains the same for all members of all families at all times. They are ignoring the roads that have more recently been built and the directions other families have discovered.

Jack should have a thorough examination to establish that he is not suffering from a physical illness. If he is not, he needs to be prodded and pushed back into relationships with his peers. Hopefully, his family will talk with other parents, do some reading, maybe talk a bit with a family counselor, and then encourage Jack to talk by listening to what he has to say. If they can present Jack with positive choices instead of negative ones, he will be less inclined to take refuge in illness. If they can be matter-of-fact about his physical symptoms so that he does not feel rewarded by being sick, he may give up this kind of behavior altogether.

Jack's illness and Maggie's alienation are products more of guilt than of fear. Alonzo does not feel the least bit guilty about his sexual relationships. He feels fear, which is brought on because he does not know in what way he wishes to relate to the opposite sex.

Social Roles

Everyone has to relate to other people, not just sexually but as friends, parents, employers, or employees. There are rules of behavior that govern the ways we relate. These rules are applied in different ways among different age groups and in different social situations. The same person may act quite differently at work than he or she does at home, on vacations, or at church. At work, persons may act as employees, at home as parents, on vacation as tourists, at church as worshippers. Academics call these clusters of prescribed behaviors that are appropriate to certain situations *social roles*.

Part of the job of parenting is to assist NQA's to adopt the roles that are expected of adults. These roles may be different from the roles utilized by the parents. They also may be different from the roles used by the NQA's when they were preteens or teen-agers. Learning these roles is not necessarily automatic, like growing a beard or beginning to menstruate. There is much more flexibility in social behavior than there is in physical behavior.

People do not passively behave in a way that a particular situation may try to impose upon them. They can recast situations in ways that provide them with greater satisfaction, or cause them less anguish or anxiety. Assuming a role is not like putting on a coat—the same coat each time one goes out-of-doors. Individuals can tailor their behavior to enable them to obtain what they want from situations. People can *make* roles as well as *take* roles.

Alonzo learned a sort of traditionally macho role from his natural father. This role excluded congenial relationships with women. He learned a different type of role from his stepfather, that of a good, loving, nice husband. This role did not satisfy Alonzo since it did not seem to include any sexual orientation. He became confused and anxious, and he has finally taken refuge in another role, which he has created for himself in reference to the opposite sex. At present, this role is providing him with some degree of satisfaction since by its use he avoids challenging situations and the suffering his anxiety causes him.

If Alonzo's mother and stepfather accept this role Alonzo has created, and define him within this role as a dutiful and loving son, it is possible that he could stay home and live with them forever. He might not be too happy, but he might not be too unhappy either since his anxiety is under control. Mother and stepfather may not be too happy, but they may not be too unhappy either. They have someone to cut the grass and take care of the dog when they go on vacation. And "After all, you know how Al is."* This demonstrates one way that a hazard can be eliminated. It can be defined out of existence. This often happens and works well when all parties are comfortable in their roles and don't attempt to change them at a later date.

However, Alonzo's mother and stepfather are disturbed by his behavior. They want him to become more independent. They may be able to help Alonzo redefine his role by talking with him and providing him with more information about various aspects of their relationship—their adult roles.

In Alonzo's case, another possibility exists—a crisis may occur. Perhaps his mother and stepfather will initiate the crisis by requesting that he move somewhere else. There is a good chance that this might shake him out of his present sets

---

*This seemingly innocuous phrase, which is heard so often, is an example of role definition. It can have undesirable side effects since it makes escape from a particular role almost impossible.

of behavior regarding the opposite sex, or confirm him further in them.

Cherie's parents have chosen certain roles for her. These include being the most popular of girls, doing well academically, and eventually marrying happily (naturally, to a socially acceptable young man). They have been guiding her step by step through the maze. Turn left here, Cherie. Now take three giant steps and turn right. Because they manipulated circumstances and situations so well, Cherie was confident that she too would march to the center of the maze, head held high and all banners waving. When she ran into unexpected obstacles, she was unprepared to cope with them, and, to make it worse, now she isn't sure that the center of the maze as described by her parents is just where she wants to go. She is not sure because she is not used to thinking for herself, but she is beginning to suspect that her goals and her parents' goals are not quite the same. Since she loves and respects her parents and knows that they try to do what is best for her, she has decided that there must be something wrong with her.

All persons take roles that are imposed upon them by the social situation, such as mother, daughter, sweetheart, student, wife. Simultaneously, they adapt these roles to suit their own aspirations. Cherie's parents expect her to take a role that fulfills *their* aspirations. The parents' aspirations are unrealistic for two reasons. They want their child to be perfect. Since this goal is unattainable, it dooms her to failure, at least in some areas. The second reason is that Cherie has aspirations for herself. She is not merely a passive role taker. She is also a role maker for herself. This illustrates some reasons behind the most common hazard that families face during the NQA years—the conflict between role taking and role making. Because Cherie's parents are important to her, she is having difficulties working out the contradiction that the conflict generates. She wants to control herself, to make her own role, to achieve her own goals. She also wants to make Mom and Dad proud of her.

Cherie needs her parents' help to free herself of their unrealistic goals for her. She needs to seek alternative routes to the center of the maze, and she needs to have their assurance that they will love and respect her both as their daughter and as an autonomous adult.

One thing she does not need is to have her parents allow her to wallow in self-pity. "Tsk! Tsk! Poor Cherie!" coming from Mom and Dad would confirm her in her feelings of failure. Her parents can help Cherie by confirming her autonomy, by showing they respect her ability to make choices for herself. The one choice she cannot be permitted is to hang around the house saying, "I'm a worthless person." That role involves the parents too, and they control their own roles in the home. They don't have to become martyrs to Cherie's depression.

One of the most encouraging characteristics of the hazards with which we have been dealing is that they tend to be *self-limiting*; that is, they tend to diminish with time. So, during the NQA period, the most important attitude for parents to maintain is that of optimism. If family relationships are maintained, no matter how difficult or tenuous they may be at times, the passage of time will allow the working through of most of the hazards. A hazard may not entirely disappear, but it can be managed with a minimum of discomfort and unhappiness.

A sense of hope for the future is an important characteristic for parents and for NQA's. This hope will diminish any effects of the hazards that occur during the NQA period.

REFERENCES

[1] Erik H. Erikson, *Childhood and Society* (New York: W.W. Norton and Co., 1963), pp. 261-63.
[2] Erikson, *Identity, Youth and Crisis* (New York: W.W. Norton, and Co., 1968), pp. 18-19.
[3] A. Freud, "Adolescence," in *Adolescence: Contemporary Studies*, eds. A. Winder and D. Angus (New York: American Books, 1968), pp. 13-24.

[4]J. Conger, *Adolescence and Youth* (New York: Harper and Row Pub. Co., Inc., 1973), Chap. I.

[5]T. Gordon, *P.E.T. Parent Effectiveness Training* (New York: New American Library, 1975).

[6]Conger, *Adolescence*, Chaps. 13, 14.

[7]H. Katchadurian, "Medical Perspectives on Adulthood," *Daedulus, Journal of American Academy of Arts and Sciences* (Spring 1976).

[8]*Ibid.*

[9]S. Hersh, "Suicide," *MH, The Magazine of the National Association for Mental Health* (Summer 1975).

FOR ADDITIONAL READING

GLASSER, W., *Reality Therapy*. New York: Harper & Row, 1975.

Useful in providing a contemporary approach to emotional distress from a medical point of view.

KLAGSBURN, F., *Too Young to Die: Youth and Suicide*. Boston: Houghton Mifflin, 1976.

A potpourri of Freudian theory on suicide, what to do, suicide centers; overemphasizing the responsibility of the family for the suicidal act.

KLINE, N., *From Sad to Glad*. New York: Ballantine Books, 1975.

An easy-to-read book, helpful in understanding depression. Overemphasis on drug therapy.

PARK, C., and L. SHAPIRO, *You Are Not Alone*. Boston: Little, Brown, and Co., 1976.

Especially useful in aiding understanding of mental difficulties and upsets. Gives very practical suggestions on community resources for assistance; how to deal with mental health professionals, the law, hospitals; talks about money problems in relation to mental difficulties. Most importantly, describes the resources available in individuals and families to deal with the situation.

TENNOV, D., *The Hazardous Cure*. New York: Anchor Books, 1976.

Describes the potentials for exploitation in the psychotherapeutic encounter. Oriented toward women, but has application toward men as well.

Moving Toward Adulthood: NQA's and Career Establishment

Career is commonly defined as the development of attitudes, skills, and security in an occupation. This is an accurate, but limited definition especially when it is used in reference to individuals, as opposed to job categories. This chapter concerns the occupational career development of NQA's in the context of broader social circumstances that have an important influence on the way young people move into the labor force of our country. Keep in mind that what we have discussed in previous chapters is an important part of the careers of NQA's; unless an individual is mature in other aspects of life, it is difficult to be responsible and secure in the workaday world.

We noted in Chapter 4, when discussing the financial aspects of career development, that young people from childhood on are encouraged to think about "what they are going to be" when they grow up. Young people are led to believe that career establishment will be a metamorphosis—at some set time they will cease to be dependent upon the family and will, like the sudden change from cocoon to butterfly, be launched on a successful career.

Career establishment, like any other aspect of life, is a gradual process of development that begins in childhood and extends through adulthood. For most people, it is impossible to predict what the future will be with more than a small degree of certainty. Only a few move into the careers they dreamed about when they were children. The future is dictated by the present. Present events must be managed and implications drawn for the future. Too great an emphasis on the future can lead to the neglect of the present. Parents and NQA's may then miss present opportunities that enable young people to exert influence on what they are becoming.

High school graduates have a good idea of the occupational fields that exist today, such as health, government, military, education, banking, production, distribution, advertising. But their ideas of the positions they may hold in these fields are romanticized and minimally differentiated. They are trendy in their job choices; in the 1960s they wanted to be astronauts, today they may want to be researchers. Very few want to be "just a secretary." Many want to "be their own boss." The unrealistic hopes and limited understanding that high school graduates have of what is available to them in careers can lead to limitations of future career choice.

Occupational fields consist of a host of related jobs, some of which have more applicants than vacancies; others have more openings than qualified persons to fill them. This supply and demand situation is fluid, and it is not easy to keep current with the labor market. Also, each job in a large occupational category has different requirements, as well as varying periods of training. This kind of information can be obtained from the local library or the career counselor at the high school. It will be very helpful to the young person if the parents become familiar with the overall job situation when their children become interested in a certain occupation. They can assist a good deal in helping young persons think through career choices.

Parents can help young people to de-mythologize their career aspirations. One of the most important things they can do at the outset is to be sure that they are not imposing their own aspirations upon their children. This is a common and understandable issue between parents and their NQA's. Parents want their children to "have it better than I did," and by that they may mean that they want their children to move into a white collar or professional position and to make more money than they did. But that may not be what the young person wants at all, and the parents should be wise enough to realize this and to recognize it as a valid position for the NQA to hold.

Parents can also point out to their NQA's that it is almost impossible today for one to "be his or her own boss" in any occupation. Even physicians, the traditional epitome of the independent profession, are hounded by patients, drug companies, staff, insurance companies, regulatory bodies, and consumer groups to the point where they, in greater numbers than ever before, are moving into large clinics or are becoming employees of large organizations, such as hospitals, government agencies, or industry. This is the era of the large organization, and most persons are consigned to be employees of organizations. This is by no means all bad. If one prepares oneself well for this eventuality, one can achieve job security and a pleasant work experience, with some independence in carrying out one's career in the large organization. This can, in a real sense, constitute being "one's own boss."

People often also get mixed up in the social value or status that they ascribe to various jobs. "Just being a secretary" is not descriptive, but it still gives a negative definition of the job. Consider how well paid most secretaries are today; how short the supply is in relation to the demand; the variety of activities secretaries carry out in organizations; the variety of settings in which secretaries can work; the level of responsibility that can be achieved on the job; and the opening up of the field to men. Using the secretarial position as an example, if parents can insist on a descriptive approach to careers when discussing the prospects with their children, many of the myths, romanticisms, and obstacles can be removed. The result will be that NQA's can move forward toward career establishment with a minimum of trial and error.

It is difficult to understand why the practicality that is the genius of American industry—the ability to define a task and then figure out the best way to accomplish it—has not been transferred into the realm of everyday human relationships. NQA's want to "arrive" at being a researcher, for instance, without giving much thought about what is entailed in getting there. Is the reward worth the price of attainment; will the attainment bring the satisfactions envisioned? Parents seldom investigate either their own or their NQA's ambitions to foresee whether their children have the ability or perseverance to achieve the career ambition; whether the financial investment is within the means of the family; whether opportunities are likely to exist at the time the NQA's are ready to enter the job market; whether the NQA's will be satisfied in that particular career position. The romanticized, fairy tale approach to careers, where everyone lives happily ever after, has little place in the process of finding one's life work, if the process is to be maturing and rewarding. Yet the fairy tale attitude pervades much of the dreams that parents and NQA's have toward the NQA's career establishment.

Let's look at Tandy's career problems. For as long as she had been watching cop shows on television, Tandy wanted to be a police officer. Her parents could not understand why Tandy wanted to do this. They were certain she could never get this type of job because all the persons they knew on police forces were men. Besides, they thought being a police officer was not a prestigious occupation, like being a doctor or even a schoolteacher. And they certainly wanted Tandy to "have it better than we did," so they tried to dissuade her from pursuing this occupational aspiration. When Tandy pointed out to her parents that there were policewomen in the shows on TV, they pooh-poohed the shows as unrealistic trash.

About a year before she graduated, Tandy talked to the career counselor at the high school about going into the police field. The counselor gave Tandy some material on police and law enforcement and told her to visit the chief of the local police department. Tandy took the materials home and asked her mother if she would be interested in going with her to visit the police chief. At first her mother held back; she was wary of police ("You only see them when you're in trouble"). But, at Tandy's insistence, she finally agreed to go along. The chief couldn't see them, but he did arrange for them to see the juvenile officer.

In the meantime, Tandy and her mother read the materials the counselor had given them. They were surprised to find that police officers were a part of a much larger occupational field called law enforcement, and that within law enforcement were many opportunities with differing entrance requirements and differing job responsibilities. They were also surprised at the many opportunities for women opening up in the field. Tandy noticed that after this her mother began to change her attitude toward Tandy's aspirations. She even said she was interested in what the juvenile officer would have to say. Her father began to ask questions at the dinner table about what Tandy really wanted to do as a "cop." Even though her father couldn't bring himself to say policewoman, Tandy was encouraged about his questions, and she told him about the different things people in this field do. She said that being a police person is only one part of a large and important field. Her father listened, and for the first time he did not talk down her choice.

Tandy and her mother were interested to find that the juvenile officer had gone to school for two years beyond high school to learn to be a specialist in working with what he called "young offenders." Here were many different unfamiliar terms being used that Tandy wanted to know about. The juvenile officer also said that many of the jobs in law enforcement required a college education, and that there was a good chance that a good student could get financial assistance.

Tandy was ecstatic and could not wait to get home to tell Dad. When he heard the story, he "harrumphed" a bit, but said nothing. Tandy knew he was impressed when her mother said that Dad had told a neighbor that his daughter was going into a new and important field that was something like being a policeman, but it was much more difficult and required much more learning than just being "a cop." Tandy knew then that it would all work out and that maybe she could even count on some financial support from her parents when she went to college.

Tandy is a member of a nice, average, normal, middle-class family. Her parents are concerned about her future and want the best for her. But one can see that even in typical families like Tandy's, problems can arise around career choices. When young people express occupational aspirations in fields where parents have little knowledge, parents are forced to fall back on common sense knowledge about the field. This knowledge is often sketchy, full of errors, and stereotyped. NQA's will do well to find out as much as they can about the fields in which they are interested, not only to inform themselves, but also to inform their parents. Tandy managed her situation nicely. It could have approached crisis proportions if she had not been able to inform her parents, if her parents had not been openminded, or if Tandy had had doubts herself about what she wanted to do.

Goals and Aspirations

Most people talk about occupational *goals* rather than *aspirations*, and this is not accidental. People concentrate on the arrival point in human relationships, rather than on the means to get there. Tandy was fortunate that she had an occupational *aspiration* and not only an occupational *goal*. She was able to concentrate on how to *get to be* a police officer, rather than *being* a police officer. And because she had this approach, she was able to figure out *what to do* each step of the way.

The difference between goals and aspirations is like what is printed on a box of cake flour. On the front is a picture of a gorgeous cake that makes one's mouth water (goal), but how to get from the flour to the cake? One must turn to the side of the box and read the small print, which gives a recipe (aspiration). These detailed instructions tell how to use the flour in the box, along with other ingredients, which one must collect from a variety of sources. Only by doing what the recipe says can one arrive at the goal of the gorgeous cake.

Aspirations are necessary to the attainment of goals because aspirations not only include where one may want to go, but they also contain a recipe for getting there. The problem is that occupational aspirations are more complicated than the aspiration to bake a cake. Most NQA's occupational aspirations are like a box of cake flour with a beautiful picture of the cake on all sides, but no recipe as to how to bake it. Career aspirations include the end product, the plan to get there, and carrying out the plan. So, in the gradual but important process of career establishment, NQA's should concentrate both on where they want to end up and how they propose to arrive at that occupational position. Parents are important participants in this process.

There is no way to go to the corner store, pick out a career aspiration kit, and then put it all together so that the young person will automatically be an adult with an established career. NQA's must, on a trial-and-error basis, work out what they want to be.

Risks in Career Establishment

Anything as uncertain as the process of career establishment can be involves risks on the part of NQA's and parents alike. Risks create fear and hesitation. NQA's want to be sure that they will become what they want to be. Parents want any investment they make to pay off. If NQA's play it safe, they will probably take the first job that comes along after graduation from high school. They may have that same job, if they don't get fired, when they retire. But the difficulty is, they probably will not want to fry hamburgers or whatever for 40 years. And if they did, they wouldn't be able to live on their wages anyway.

So, to take advantage of the opportunities that exist about them, NQA's take risks and make investments of time, energy, and money, even though no certainty exists that the investments will pay off as desired. This is hard for NQA's *and* parents. In fact, the greater the career ambition, the greater the risks that are involved. What are some of these risks?

NQA's may spend years in study, and spend large amounts of their own and their parents' money, and not be able to get a job in their field when they are ready. The person with a Ph.D. in English is a case in point. There are many more Ph.D.'s produced in English each year than there are jobs open to graduates. Or a person may study for medical school and not get admitted. Some people obtain jobs in their chosen fields and dislike the job intensely when it does not turn out as they thought it would. These risks are unpleasant to contemplate and can cause disappointment and suffering.

But consider the alternatives.

A completely safe society is a society where no choice is possible. A society where failure is eliminated is a society where success is unknown. A society where poverty is eradicated is a society where fortunes cannot be made. A society where completely safe cars are mandated is a society where cars are all alike, and choice becomes no choice at all. No mountains could be climbed, no suggestions for change would be tolerated, because climbing mountains and making changes involve taking risks. In a completely safe society, no opportunities are available, no choices exist.

The situation today is between the extremes of the completely safe society and what was more nearly the characteristic of the "good old days." The risks were tremendous then, and too few were able to profit from risk taking, but those who did, such as Carnegie, Rockefeller, and Vanderbilt, really made it big.

Today, people can still take risks; opportunities are still available. At the same time, failure is not as final as it used to be. Security of some sort is all but guaranteed, and outstanding individual success, although not impossible, is rarer and more difficult to come by.

Today, parents can be reasonably certain that their children will do as well occupationally as they did, and perhaps even achieve a higher career position. NQA's still can try a variety of jobs and career lines, lines that often as not are different from those picked while in high school. The NQA period, although extending the duration of parent–child relationships, also has advantages in that NQA's have a longer period in which to experiment with career choices. Few families yet recognize this advantage. The NQA period is important, for it permits the family to continue its contribution to the transformation of the child into the adult. An important mark of the adult is that the adult is occupationally secure and, therefore, financially independent.

Social Changes and Career Establishment

We often hear NQA's say that they do not understand why they can't find jobs since more persons are in the labor force than ever before. Contradictory as it may seem, this is why NQA's have such a difficult time getting started, and it is the primary reason for the existence of the NQA period.

Not many years ago, one third of the women in this country had some kind of gainful employment outside the home. Today, the figure has risen to 43%.[1] People are living longer. Senior citizens have organized their efforts to remove the age restrictions of mandatory retirement at 65. The handicapped are pressing for greater work opportunities. Inflation has increased the urgency for many workers to moonlight to prevent a reduction of their standard of living. A television news account gave the example of the 18-or 19-year-old man who, upon applying for a part-time job, found out he had lost it to his father, who had been given the job just a few minutes earlier. This was the father's second job. Although it meant more money for the NQA's family, it was sure to have had a discouraging effect on the motivation of the NQA.

All these developments are transforming the composition of the labor force. This blocks opportunities for early entry into the work world, and it leads to the delineation and extension of the NQA period. When entry into the labor force is blocked, young persons tend to resort to attendance in college, or other training institutions with the hope that it will expand their career opportunities later.

Adult members of society, especially those who receive the greatest benefit from keeping things as they are, fear the potential for disruption that young people possess. To prevent this from happening, certain social provisions appear that are directed at the NQA years. Public works programs, job corps, summer work programs, subsidies to businesses to create new positions, and extended unemployment benefits to discharged service people are examples of provisions made to prevent unrest among those in the NQA years.

This is a very brief discussion of some complicated changes that are taking place in the American society. These changes have great impact on all individuals. Not all individuals in the society benefit from these changes. They take place because a collective judgment is made that more individuals will benefit than not, and thus, the society will benefit. NQA's as a group suffer some negative consequences of these changes, the most notable being their extended dependence on the family, their uncertainties in career establishment, and the protraction of the period before they become fully recognized adults. They are caught in the crossfire of conflicting social forces; legal adulthood at age 18 in most states and problems of obtaining employment, which should be one of the accompaniments of legal adulthood.

People often have difficulty identifying the processes in their social surroundings that have as important an effect on them as the ones we have been describing. These processes develop slowly, are somewhat impersonal because they do not affect us directly like a birth in the family, and are difficult to relate to other social circumstances because they affect so many persons in so many different ways. The processes are uneven. Their relationship to other social circumstances is unclear. Sometimes the results are felt even before the processes are identified. The appearance of the NQA's is an example of this phenomenon.

If it were easier to identify and define what is going on in the society about us, and understand what the implications of the processes are for the future, all of us would be spared mistakes, grief, disappointment, and unprofitable ventures. But we also would be deprived of the unpredictability of life, which gives it much of its excitement and anticipation. Parents, other relatives, neighbors, and teachers would place less pressure on young persons to decide while in high school what they are going to be. They would realize the disparity that can arise between early goals, later aspirations, and the possibilities of achievement. They would see that the major advantage to being an NQA is that NQA's are spared the immediacy of being forced into unrewarding work. And what is the hurry? With the increase in life expectancy, NQA's probably will be in the labor force as long as their seniors, even though they may enter at a later date. NQA's can take some of their years outside the labor force at the young end instead of at the old end.

Adults become envious of the leisure time that NQA's have at their disposal, of their freedom from the discipline and monotony of work. So they tend to brand them as irresponsible. From this perspective, adults pressure young persons to "decide what you want to be," to believe that "fulfillment comes from work," to "choose a meaningful career that brings personal rewards and not just economic security." Adults and young persons alike know that most people work to make enough money to live, and for very few other reasons—yet the charade of fulfillment goes on.

Young people struggle to make the career decision as soon as they can, and then parents, teachers, and the young persons themselves all become upset when circumstances do not permit the NQA's to enter that career as soon as possible. This lack of opportunity to translate goals into realistic aspirations can have drastic consequences for parents and NQA's alike. This is an important factor behind the appearance of the hazards discussed in the previous chapter. It may even result in the NQA's inability ever to enter the labor force in a productive and satisfying way.

Other difficulties can arise. Young people can become so overwhelmed with the apparent career possibilities paraded before them that they are unable to define for themselves just what line of work they want. They either flit from job to job, holding one only long enough to earn some money to live on, or they lose the motivation necessary to establish themselves in a career.

Role ambiguity is another characteristic of the current social situation that creates difficulty. Role ambiguity means that there is contrast between the traditional work roles of men and women and their work roles today. When we look at this situation over a span of time, we find dramatic changes taking place. Not too many decades ago, it was possible to state with authority that the woman's place was in the home. Likewise, the man was to be the breadwinner. One could fairly easily list work roles for women, such as maid, housekeeper, housewife, governess; most all having to do with domestic activities. Occupational categories were limited for women, in contrast to men who had many job classifications open to them. There was little crossover of women into male work roles.

The situation is different today. The barriers are lowered, and women are beginning to move into work activities not long ago the exclusive territory of men. Men are also beginning to take on more domestic responsibilities about the home, once the exclusive domain of women. We witness a mixing of traditional work specialization. It is no longer possible to predict with relative accuracy what categories of work activities are available to young persons on the basis of their sex.

But work roles are still defined in terms of sexual specialization. This is what is meant when it is said that women are moving into men's jobs. There is also the reverse, however—men moving into the traditional work sphere of women, such as nursing and secretarial work, although not to the same extent as the opposite trend. In many cases, when women do enter the work force, they do not give up their domestic responsibilities in the home, but add their employment tasks to their other activities. However, increased sharing of work in the home between men and women is taking place.

So, young people have available to them today a much wider range of career choices than was previously the case. Three major categories of career choices exist:

1. Traditional female career roles. These are still defined as such, but men are also entering these jobs.
2. Traditional male career roles. Women, in increasingly large numbers, are acquiring jobs in this category.
3. Integrated career roles. Men and women are rearranging the old work specialization lines, sharing activities that were recently segregated by sex.

The freedom to move into such a wide variety of career lines makes it more difficult for young persons to know what it means to be a woman, to be a man. Can one be feminine and be a steelworker? Can one be masculine and be a social worker? If one wants to marry, and both marriage partners want to work, who is the principal breadwinner, how are the domestic responsibilities allocated? Can one be masculine or feminine and be a homosexual? Even if some answers to these questions can be found, what career lines should young persons pick for themselves? Choice involves problems, especially at present when new patterns have not yet emerged sufficiently to guide young persons in their decisions.

The wider range of choices for careers available today places NQA's in an interesting position. They are to be envied for having this freedom; yet they are to be supported in their efforts to plot direction and take steps to establish themselves in careers. With choices come trial and error, at least until career lines become more clarified than they now are. This situation accentuates the NQA period, for NQA's will be dependent upon their parents at least to some degree while they are trying a number of the career lines in the effort to establish themselves as adults.

This chapter has discussed mainly career lines where young people prepare themselves for employment in establishments that they do not own. But this is also an issue in family-owned businesses. It is no longer automatic that the business either goes to the oldest son or is shared among the sons; daughters can now also compete for succession. If a daughter does obtain control of the business over sons, questions arise for which there are no easy answers, such as determination of career lines for the other children, length of financial dependence upon the parents, and problems of relationships among members of the family.

A friend who is a keen observer said recently, "It used to be that people had nervous breakdowns in their forties, but now it's coming during the twenties. Oh, well, that's probably best, they'll get it out of the way early." Little wonder, with the role ambiguity that currently exists.

We have described the importance that changes in procedures of career establishment play in the emergence of the NQA period. Difficulties inherent in change of this nature were pointed out, but the increased opportunities that such change also brings were emphasized. There are certain considerations to keep in mind that can minimize the difficulties. For instance, when NQA's find a field in which they are interested, check out the job options within it, weigh the odds of job opportunities, job satisfaction, time and expense of training, rewards available, and future trends in the field. Even if some of the results seem negative, try not to play it too safe. The future is not all that predictable; the NQA may draw to an inside straight. NQA's have more chance to succeed in a career they find fascinating, no matter how crowded, than in one they take only because there are many jobs available.

If the NQA makes a false start? With the time NQA's have available, they can make several starts and not be bad off in the long run. There is an average of five career shifts before age 30. Parents can assist NQA's to develop another plan for career development. Hazards of failure can be avoided if abortive career attempts are seen as a normal process of career establishment. Concentrate on the opportunities; emphasize the strengths that NQA's have rather than their weakness. Define success and failure in the NQA's terms. Try to understand the NQA's interests and capabilities. Remember, though, that this is not the same as letting NQA's have their own way.

And, finally, it is comforting to realize that NQA's have greater opportunity than previous generations to experiment in career establishment. So much of one's lifetime is committed to work; if NQA's can, with the freedom of time and enlarged choices, obtain greater personal satisfaction from work, everyone will be better off for it.

REFERENCES

[1] Women's Bureau, U.S. Department of Labor, 1974.

FOR ADDITIONAL READING

BOLLES, R., *What Color Is Your Parachute?* Berkeley, Calif.: Ten Speed Press, 1975.

Discusses in a lively style the in's and out's, the why's and where-fore's, of career selection and job choice.

MALNIG, L., and S. MORROW, *What Can I Do With a Major In . . .?* Jersey City, N.J.: St. Peter's College Press, 1975.

Gives useful information on what types of jobs can be obtained, depending on the major subject of the college student or recent graduate.

STANAT, K., and P. REARDON, *Job Hunting Secrets and Tactics.* Chicago: Follett Corp., 1977.

Gives specific suggestions, easily understood, on how to get a job once the decision has been made to seek it.

U.S. GOVT. PRINTING OFFICE, *Guide to Federal Career Literature*, 1976.

Sourcebook for published information concerning career lines and job opportunities at all levels of the federal government.

Moving Toward Adulthood: Establishing Adult Relationships Between Children and Parents

Most people have all they can do to deal with present situations. They don't think too much about what their present acts might mean for the future. Only after the future becomes the present can people see any links between the series of decisions they made about their lives.

Having children is a prime example. Few people give much thought to the investment of time, money, or emotion that children will require. At the time that children arrive on the scene, few parents can be very explicit about the reasons they desire them or what they expect from the experience of parenting. When children are about to leave home, parents can usually give some general reasons for having had children, but these reasons are not very original. They consist of ideas taken from folk wisdom and traditions, or explanations developed in an earlier age. Parents often give blank stares when asked to list some reasons why they had children—their goals and aspirations for parenting. A number of commonly accepted reasons for having children do come forth in conversations and from writings about parenthood. These are condensed into nine categories, which we will call the traditional goals of parenting.

Traditional Goals of Parenting

Economic Reward

Economic reward is a somewhat surprising goal that parents list; except in rare circumstances, children today are an economic drain. When labor was more closely related to the home, children were an economic advantage since they furnished a labor pool. However, as industrialization proceeded and labor was concentrated in large organizations such as factories, plants, businesses, and industrial farms, children were needed less and less to do the work for the family. The responsibility for furnishing the family resources has fallen more and more on the parents, with children being economically dependent on them until the time they leave home.

But parents state that children can still offer assistance in an emergency, and they guarantee security in old age. This is usually beyond the means of most children, who are then themselves trying to cope with the expenses of maintaining their own homes and families. Because of this situation, public programs for support of older persons have developed within the last half-century. Economic benefits from children are difficult to find in today's age.

Societal Perfection

This goal of parenting is quite old, but it still has currency. Through proper training, children will avoid the mistakes of their parents; by observing the mess society is in presently, they will do things better. Children are presumed to have the ability to change the existing patterns of societal relationships and to have some prescience about the future that previous generations lacked.

Throughout history, numbers of utopian groups have sprung up that are convinced they have the answer to the problems of existence, either on this earth or the next. Many of these groups—religious, political, ethnic—reason that if they can produce enough children who are imbued with the particular utopian beliefs, the children can both convert others and populate the earth with true believers through their own children. Through these means, society can bit by bit become better than it is at present.

Immortality

The line of descent, the family tree, the continuance of the family name are important to many people, and only through children can these goals be met. Our society is more secular than in previous times. Not everyone believes in the hereafter promised by organized religion, so the search for immortality now takes a different turn. When life for the individual stops at death, the only way the individual can live on is through offspring. This may be the force behind the current movement to trace geneology; to find "roots;" to make certain that what came from one's genes will be transmitted to the future through children.

Biological Fulfillment

Some people (men *and* women) say that they had a bodily urge to have children, which they feel is innate to the organism. Women add that they would never have been satisfied without the physical experience of childbirth; the carrying of the child in the womb, the early feeding of the newborn.

Self-Fulfillment

These parents live their lives to rear their children. Children are the instruments of parental satisfaction. The joys, sorrows, achievements, failures of children are those of the parents. "Susan and George are going to be leaving home shortly, and I don't know what I am going to do when they're gone. Life will be so empty."

Protection from Loneliness

This goal is related to the one above. The "empty nest syndrome" results when children are gone from the home, and parents have not developed interests for themselves to substitute for the demands that children previously made. Parents also state that they hope that children can protect them from the loneliness of old age. Some parents use the companionship of their children as a substitute for an absent, unsatisfactory, or distant mate.

Create the Perfect Child

This goal is based upon the assumption that children at birth have a general potential that is later channeled into specific behavior by experiences and training. It is also based on the assumption that parents are the only influence in the lives of their children. And, finally, it is thought that children have little ability to determine their own behavior for themselves. Parents believe that they can mold their children's personalities, "create a perfect child." Many books and countless articles reinforce these assumptions. Parents believe that to do this they must be competent, perfect or nearly perfect themselves, powerful, and, above all, responsible. It also bespeaks a certain arrogance on the part of parents—they will create children that will not make the mistakes others make—they are omnipotent and omniscient. When parents recognize that it is not possible to achieve this goal, they often react with strong feelings of guilt, bitterness, and cynicism toward those who led them to believe in the goal, and they begin to doubt their own adequacy.

The Proper Technique

This will yield the proper response in the child. This goal is closely related to the goal of creating the perfect child. It is a direct outgrowth of the important social value of progress through technology. "Progress is our most important product," says General Electric. And the progress comes through research into better productive processes. Parents often state, "If we had only known how, we could have helped Johnny," or "If we could only go to someone to teach us the perfect approach, we wouldn't have these problems with Annie." Printing presses still churn out tons of writings that tell parents that if they would spend more time with Bill, let Sam be himself, feed Marjory this diet, attend that class on parenthood, their problems with their children would disappear. Few family watchers discuss the fact that these little creatures may have minds of their own, which give them the capability to direct their own behaviors and respond in their own ways to techniques of control; perhaps if only to resist the control itself.

Status

Parents are so proud when they can point to "our daughter, the doctor," or "our son, the basketball player." Parents often hope that their children can attain an economic level above what the parents have been able to reach. This will bring greater respectability in the eyes of the community; comfort, happiness, and an increase in the material conveniences of life. This goal of parents for upward mobility for their children is a powerful one in our society. The acceptance of this goal by parents and children is what makes work so important in the lives of many of our citizens.

Traditional Goals and NQA's

Traditional goals are based upon a number of long-standing assumptions about the nature of children. These goals, although admirable in character, are seldom, if ever, attainable, nor were they in the past. Those who unrealistically insist upon the attainment of traditional goals are the very same persons who predict the demise of the family. In the chapter on control and authority, we noted that children are considered to be the property of their parents until they reach the age of majority. This assumption is one upon which traditional goals are based. Two others also underlie the traditional goals; namely, children are analogous to plants or blank sheets of paper, and children are like prodigals, the repositories of original sin.

Seedlings, if watered and fertilized properly, will grow into healthy, productive adult plants. Likewise children! A blank sheet of paper takes on the characteristics of the words and sentences that are imprinted upon it. Likewise children! But, even though families do their best to raise their children into good adults, children are contrary. They often reject the admonitions of parents in favor of the evils of the world. Those who believe in these anologies advocate that, to overcome this problem, either the family must be strengthened or the world must be made better, or both.

Many of the traditional goals of parenting are couched in modern, scientific terminology, which disguises the fact that they have been with us for a long time. Behaviorism is a prominent modern example of the application of the quaint analogy of plants and blank sheets of paper. In general, behaviorism holds that those who are charged with the care of children in our society, such as parents, teachers, and other child-care professionals, can elicit predictable responses from children by providing appropriate stimuli. When children do not respond in accordance with pre-established goals, the persons in charge of children must alter the stimuli to modify the behavior of the children.

Mead[1] and Bronfenbrenner,[2] who illustrate the third analogy, tend to view children as prodigals, caught between the "good" family and the "evil" world. Family watchers such as these are concerned that parents are rendered ineffectual because of erosion of the elements of society that previously have supported the socialization of children so that they would turn out in accordance with one or more of the traditional goals. Parents are not doing a very adequate job, but it is not really their fault. They are prevented from going so because of social changes, usually described as negative, that dissipate their control over their children. And children, being what they are, exploit this erosion of control to flaunt the traditional goals. The point of view of these kinds of family watchers is pessimistic, and, if accepted, can lead one to a rather grim view of the future of the family, as well as succeeding generations of adults in America.

Traditional goals are derived exclusively from society, administered by parents and other persons charged with care of children. Traditional goals assume that children are passive receptacles of socialization. When the older child or young adult does not turn out in accordance with traditional goals, the responsibility for this failure is placed either upon the persons caring for the children, the children themselves, or both. The goals themselves are not questioned, only the individuals involved. When the goals are not reached, the characteristics of the family are attacked; parents are blamed, children are reproached.

Children, however, have an active rather than a passive part to play in their movement toward adulthood. Children have as much to do with how they turn out as do parents, teachers, and other persons who influence the movement toward adulthood. It is a joint endeavor. By the time children reach the NQA period, they have a well-developed sense of who they are, and they exert considerable control over what they do. If NQA's are not granted this individuality of existence, they will seize it for themselves. In other words, NQA's have choices obvious to them. Oftentimes these choices are in direct opposition to traditional goals. When parents insist upon implementation of traditional goals, an adversary relationship will likely ensue. With choices available, self-control is exerted. When NQA's see a variety of possibilities open to them and are faced with parents who adhere to traditional goals, a power struggle will develop between parents and children, a struggle neither side can decisively win. The emergence of the NQA period gives parents and children alike the opportunity to pool resources to provide a transition for children from adolescence to adulthood. The emergence of the NQA period is also evidence of continued vitality of the family and the society, not, as some would have us think, a sign of disorganization and disintegration. Continuing adaptation of relationships between parents and their children is required as children move toward adulthood.

Reaching Beyond Traditional Goals

Adaptation does not require that the past be invalid. The opposite is true—the past is essential, and parents are the ones to whom NQA's turn to find out how things were done "when you were young, Mom and Dad." It is not possible for parents to erase the past; it is their experiences that have made them what they are. But to make the past meaningful for NQA's, parents will need to know the nature of the world in which their NQA's live, and this means listening to their NQA's. Parents should not assume that because of their years of experience, they know it all and can teach it to their NQA's. The opposite may be true. Thus, instead of parents proceeding from a traditional perspective, and NQA's concluding that their parents are old fuddy-duddies, each can learn from the other. In this way, parents can consider their NQA's more adult than adolescent, and act toward them as adults in every way possible. NQA's can consider their parents as not being out-of-date or dictatorial, but being an important source of knowledge and wisdom to link the present to the past and thus increase life's meaning for all members of the family. Parents and NQA's can become a group of adults related to each other in a unique way, rather than as a continuation of earlier child–parent patterns.

Traditional goals assume that the future will be the same as the past, and thus certain. But with the choices that are available for NQA's, the future is not all that predictable. This implies that problems will arise, events will take unanticipated turns, difficult choices will become apparent. But, with the point of view of the inevitability of some uncertainty, parents and NQA's can work together to develop plans for the future.

Traditional goals make no provision for activities when the goals are met, when the condition is reached. Parents often ask, "How can I give up these goals? What will I replace them with?" Letting go means replacing the goals that included direct care for NQA's with other goals in life. This cannot be done without consideration of the future with the NQA physically gone from the family. What will Mom do when she no longer has to cook for more persons than herself and Dad? When the children are gone, how will the time be filled? If a child is killed, or dies, how will the family continue? With increased longevity, what will parents do with the many years left beyond the child-rearing ones?

How can NQA's shift from having Mom and Dad figure things out for them to doing that for themselves? To whom can NQA's go when they are no longer at home and get in a jam? How do they feed and clothe themselves? The NQA period gives families time to anticipate these questions and come up with ways to proceed that are more than hasty improvisations. "Playing it by ear" results in too many mistakes and unwarranted disappointments.

In the last chapter, we discussed goals and aspirations. We said that goals are the end point of any activity, and aspirations involve ways, means, and processes by which goals are reached. Goals once reached must then be succeeded by other goals. But aspirations can remain constant. Parents can continue to aspire that their children will be successful, long after they transcend their NQA years. NQA's can continue to aspire that their parents will be content, and that Mom or Dad also will continue to be successful, long after NQA's no longer live in the family. Even as it is important that parents and NQA's learn goal succession, it is important that parents and NQA's retain constant aspirations for each other. When all members of the family of origin become adults, aspirations for each other will become nearly identical.

The NQA Years—Toward the Goal of Expanding Family Relationships

Many family watchers survey the contemporary scene and conclude that the family is shrinking in composition and contribution. They claim that the extended family is finished, that the nuclear family is beset by external forces that threaten its viability.[3] Families *do* face contemporary challenges, but we see the trend toward expanding family relationships. And it is mainly because of modern technology that this is now possible.

The usual concept of the extended family is based on the agrarian assumption of geographical proximity, which was the case to some extent in previous decades. When the family watchers note geographical mobility of people, they assume that the extended family is weakened because geographical separation used to mean relational weakening. But consider the case of individuals in earlier times who left home to create their own families and fortunes in distant locations, perhaps across oceans or continents. Travel was difficult, communication no easier, and time and resources for contact with the family of origin were scarce. Was the extended family a relationship that only a minority of our citizens could enjoy prior to advanced developments in transportation and communication, instead of being the organizational rule usually stated as true? The nuclear family was also common during the nineteenth century and the early decades of the twentieth.

Advancements in travel and communication make it convenient and affordable for people to stay in touch with each other either by telephone or by visiting. The current trend is the reverse of earlier times where, when children left home, parents often lost track of them forever. Children may still be separated by long geographical distances. Everyday one hears advertisements on the radio and television, or reads in the newspaper, that one can call anywhere in the United States for less than $2.00. One mother discussed her fears about her daughter moving to another state. She was gone from the family forever, the mother lamented. When asked if she ever heard from her daughter, the mother said, "Oh, yes. We talk to each other by phone at least once a week." Was the daughter on her own? "Oh, I send her some money every once in a while, when she says she needs some," answered the mother. "And she will be home for a visit at Easter." That does not sound like a "lost child." This example is typical of situations in families where children are moving through the NQA years.

This emerging pattern of continuation of familial relationships on such a large scale past the adolescent and early adult years is a contributing factor to the emergence of the NQA period. There must be a period where relationships are modified from those of the earlier periods of childhood and adolescence, a period where children are concentrating to become adults, where parents and children are gradually diluting the intensity of relationships and preparing themselves for relationships based more on the availablity of technologies for their continuance. This is all done during the NQA years. This fact leads to the necessity for the redefinition of relationships that we have concentrated on throughout this book.

Letting Go and Getting Free—
Toward the Goal of Establishing
the Mature Natural Family

The major theme of this book is that an extension of relationships between parents and children is in progress in our society. In the mature, natural family, all members are adults. We have used many pages to describe the characteristics of this development and the social reasons that gave rise to it. But we do *not* intend to delineate and therefore create another period in child–family relationships to stack on top of the periods of childhood and adolescence, like layers on a cake. Most discussions of childhood and adolescence *are* like the layers on the cake—the top one depends on the lower one for its position and is practically identical to it. Adolescence grows out of childhood and is discussed most often in reference to it. In short, adolescence is oriented toward the past. We have discussed the NQA period almost solely in reference to the future. This is what makes the NQA period unique, and why it is such an important development in the history of the American family. The family in America is modifying its patterns to give continued support to its members throughout a longer span of time. This is for two reasons: to prepare the children for life in a world where increased choices exist for the future, and to prepare for continuing although less intense, relationships throughout the entire lives of all the family members.

What, then, are the relationships that the NQA years point toward when all members of the natural family are adults?

There is an egalitarianism in the mature, natural family. Children, instead of looking toward their parents for support, now can provide emotional and psychological support for their parents, similar to what the parents formerly provided for them. Adult children often assist parents with personal, physical, and financial problems. Parents find they can learn much from their adult children that can make their life fuller as they grow older. Adult children can also continue to learn from their parents. In an effective mature, natural family, parents serve as counselors and advisors, but children are free to accept or ignore the advice and counsel as they see fit. Adult children are free from the family of origin, but they are not cut off. There is a difference.

The effective mature, natural family becomes a very special reference group for its members. It creates standards, provides a source of knowledge, provides support for the creation of new families of origin by the children when they in turn marry and have their own children. The effective mature, natural family enables adult children and their offspring to develop relationships and become familiar with older adults. This is especially important as lifetimes extend and the older proportion of the population increases.

This emerging effective mature, natural family counteracts the segregative tendencies of the society that, among other things, result in unequal distribution of older adults. It furnishes information for children and grandchildren about their own futures as older adults, and thus enables them to avoid some of the difficulties that contemporary adults face. As various members of the mature, natural family observe people over two and three generations, they obtain indications about the continuity of the social order. They learn to appreciate that the present and the future each has a past.

Welcome the emergence of the NQA period. It substantiates the strength of the family. The family is responding to changes in conditions surrounding it. The American society is providing a period for families to summarize their individual histories of child rearing during the NQA period and to turn these experiences toward the future. That is the essence of letting go, of getting free; to let go of the past, to get free for the future. Parents can let go of the day-to-day responsibilities for their children and free their children to be adults as parents are. Children can let go of the dependencies of their earlier years and be free to move to adulthood, which is the reason for all that goes before.

REFERENCES

[1]M. Mead, "Can the American Family Survive?" *Redbook*. (February 1977) pp. 91, 154–61.

[2]U. Bronfenbrenner, *Two Worlds of Childhood: US and USSR* (New York: Russell Sage Foundation, 1970).

[3]Bronfenbrenner, "Nobody Home: The Erosion of the American Family," *Psychology Today* (May 1977), pp. 42–47.

FOR ADDITIONAL READING

HEWITT, JOHN, *Self and Society*. Boston: Allyn and Bacon, 1976.

> *Excellent, if textbookish, explanation of how humans progress from birth onward to become participating members of society.*

LAPIERE, R., *Social Change*. New York: McGraw Hill Pub. Co., 1965.

> *See especially the chapter on the family. Describes how the family has adapted to changing circumstances during the past 400 years.*

SHIBUTANI, T., *Society and Personality*. Englewood Cliffs, N.J.: Prentice-Hall, Inc., 1961.

> *Describes the importance of the family and other primary groups in the development of the individual. Research and examples a bit dated, but otherwise good.*

SLATER, P., *The Pursuit of Loneliness*. Boston: Beacon Press, 1970.

> *If dated references to Vietnam are ignored, the book provides useful insights into the contemporary situation.*

Index

A

Abortion, 125
Abstract thinking, 60, 61
Adoption, 125
Alienation, 110, 117, 124–27, 143
Anxiety, 117, 128–30, 139, 144
Aspirations, 152–57, 161, 162,
177–78
Authoritarianism, 16–17, 21, 25
Autonomy (*see* Control, struggle for)

B

Bankruptcy, 65
Behaviorism, 174
Bouncing checks, 63
Bronfenbrenner, U., 174
Buddy groups, 89

C

Car, use of, 8, 22–24
Career establishment, 151–65
goals and aspirations, difference between, 156–57

S

T

U

V

W